THE GOLD GUIDES

SICILY

THE COMPLETE GUIDE TO THE ISLAND

PLACES OF NATURAL BEAUTY
ART - ARCHAEOLOGY

BONECHI

© Copyright by CASA EDITRICE BONECHI
Via Cairoli, 18/b - 50131 Firenze- Italia
Tel. 055/576841 - Fax 055/5000766
E-mail: bonechi@bonechi.it
Internet: www.bonechi.it

Printed in Italy by Centro Stampa Editoriale Bonechi
Text: Giuliano Valdes, Editing Studio, Pisa
Translation: Traduco s.n.c. by Bovone e Bulckaen, Florence
Editing: Fiore Batini, Maria Grazia Parri
Layout: Sonia Gottardo
Cartography: Alessandra Martini pages 11, 37, 59, 71, 75, 91, 111, 127, 142-143;
Studio Grafico Bellandi e Mariani: pages 51, 60, 80.
Photo setting: "m & m", Florence
Plates by: La Fotolitografia, Florence

ISBN 88-7009-826-5

CREDITS

The photographs are the property of the Archives of the Casa Editrice Bonechi
and were taken by:
Marco Banti: pages: 39, 67, 69, 73, 74, 86, 87, 89, 90, 93, 95, 97, 98, 108, 109, 110, 122 top
left and bottom, 128 bottom, 129, 131, 132, 140. Gianni Dagli Orti: pages 8, 14, 15, 17, 20,
21, 23, 25, 26, 28, 29, 30, 32, 72 top, 81, 82, 83, 92, 99, 101, 102, 103. Paolo Giambone:
pages 5, 18, 31, 40, 41, 44-45, 46 top, 52, 53, 54, 55, 56, 61, 62, 63, 79, 84, 141.
Andrea Pistolesi: pages 19, 22, 124, 125 top. Giuliano Valsecchi: pages 43, middle and
bottom, 47, 48, 49, 50, 59, 64, 65, 66, 68, 72 bottom, 75, 76, 77, 78, 84, 112, 113, 114, 115,
117, 118, 119, 120, 121, 122 top right, 125 bottom, 126, 133, 134, 135, 136, 137.

Photographs by Giovanni Giunta: pages: 101, 104. Giuliano Valsecchi: pages: 6, 13, 27, 33,
34 left, 35, 36, 43 top, 105, 107, 123. Aerial photographs I-BUGA Aut. SMA n. 371/84:
pages: 12, 34 right, 38, 46 bottom, 50 right, 71, 124 bottom left, 128 top, 139. Aut. SMA
n. 850/86: p. 70. Aut. SMA n. 506/85: p. 138.

HISTORY

Ancient rock engravings have been found which seem to support the theory that the island of Sicily was joined, in the remote past, to the European continent. There are traces of Neolithic settlements, villages built of stone or on palafittes. The early inhabitants of the island included the Sicanians, who were of Iberian origin; they were followed by the Sicels, who came from various regions in southern Italy. When the first Phoenician colony was founded, there were already permanently settled areas on the island; new centres were created at Motye, Trapani, Mazara, Lilybaeum, Palermo and Solunto, and a fertile cultural and commercial interchange started up.

We have information on Greek colonies founded in Sicily as early as the eighth century B.C. This region was the most prolific in settlements in the whole territory of Magna Grecia. Greek colonies rose in rapid succession at Naxos, Catania, Leontini, Himera, Messina, Mylae, Syracuse, Megara, Gela and Agrigentum, to mention the largest and most important. In the first half of the fifth century B.C. the first large-scale war in the Mediterranean basin pitted the Syracusans against the Carthaginians, whom they defeated at Himera. The Carthaginians won back and subjected large portions of the island at the end of that century and the beginning of the next. Sicily was finally colonized by the Romans at the end of their recurring wars with Carthage, after a long and tiring campaign. The new province provided grain for the tables of the Empire, while the notorious plundering and extortions of Verres brought money and riches to the pockets of the powerful conquerors. Not until the time of Augustus was the city granted the status of civitas romana, too late to remedy the depredations of his predecessors.

The fall of the Roman Empire was followed by a rapidly changing succession of barbarian peoples (Vandals, Heruli, Goths), until the coming of the Byzantines led by Belisarius. From the ninth to the eleventh century, under the Arabs, Sicily became a Muslim territory; the Arabs left their mark on the way of life, dialectal expressions, placenames and agriculture of the island, turning it into a rich and flourishing land and making Palermo one of the most important cities in Europe.

In the second half of the eleventh century the Arabs were replaced by the Normans, who brought brilliance and luxury to the court of Palermo, promoting the artistic, economic and social development of the city.

This period of prosperity continued into the reign of Frederick II of Swabia (first half of the thirteenth century), but came to an end under his successors (his son Manfred was defeated by the Angevins at Benevento in 1266). This was the starting point for the events leading up to the Sicilian Vespers, which chased the French out of the island in 1282. The Aragonese came next, as a prelude to Sicily becoming a Spanish satellite; it became a colony of the Spanish crown until the first half of the eighteenth century.

After that time, as a pawn in the tense game being played out on the chessboard of Europe, Sicily belonged first to the house of Savoy, then to the Austrians and finally (1815) fell into the hands of the Bourbons. Repeated attempts at rebellion culminated in Garibaldi's campaign of 1860 and led to the annexation of Sicily to the new Kingdom of Italy (1861). Problems with their roots far back in the past, backwardness and centuries-old obsessions motivated recurrent insurrections against the great estates and the exploitation of the people by the barons, while lack of confidence in the state, alienation, unemployment and emigration increased. The Fascist government was unable to satisfy the just aspirations of the Sicilians, and after suffering devastation during the war, they felt betrayed and began to threaten partition; their protests were backed by increasing bandit activity (the name of Salvatore Giuliano is known to all). The central government responded by granting Sicily a special Statute, which today is still far from having solved the problems of Sicilian society, racked by the recurring spectre of Mafia terrorism and by unassuaged hopes for independence.

ART HISTORY

The first works of art produced in Sicily go back to prehistoric times. Graffiti and rock paintings have been found at the **Grotte dell'Addaura** (Palermo), in the **Grotta di S. Teodoro** (Messina) and in caves at **Cala del Genovese** (Levanzo). During the Neolithic period, while the first indigenous cultures (Stentinello, Lipari), of which many vestiges remain in ceramic and terracotta objects, were developing, relationships with the earliest forms of Aegean culture emerging in the Mediterranean basin were also increasing. The arrival of the Sicels, who imposed their culture on those already existing, was a prelude to the first influx of Phoenicians, around the eleventh century B.C., when the first colonies were founded at Palermo, Solunto and Motye.

From the eighth century B.C. on it was the turn of the Greeks, who settled on the island in several waves, leaving splendid examples of their art, which have come down to us today partly destroyed but still expressive and magnificent. As far as architecture is concerned, we have only to think of the **Theatre of Syracuse**, certainly the most important of the many in Sicily, the majestic **Temples of Agrigento and Selinunte**, the **Temple of Segesta**, the **Euryalus Castle in Syracuse** and numberless remains of ancient residences, necropolises and burial grounds. The island's museums offer rich glimpses of the painting (painted ceramics and amphoras) and sculpture; we have only to recall the marble Ephebus in the Agrigento Museum, where one of the Telamons from the Temple of Jove is also preserved, the sculptures and metopes of the temples of Selinunte (Palermo Museum) and bronzes and other carved ornaments of temple buildings (Syracuse Museum).

There are examples of the architectural heritage of the Roman colony at **Catania (Theatre, Amphitheatre), Syracuse (Amphitheatre), Palermo** (remains of houses at **Villa Bonanno**) and **Taormina** (reconstruction of the **Greek Theatre** and **Naumachia**). The exceptional series of mosaics in the **Villa Casale (Piazza Armerina)** is the most important work of decorative art, while Roman sculptures mostly inspired by Classical Greek models can be seen in the museums.

In the Norman period we find an extraordinary flowering of art, uniting and carrying to their highest level of splendour the trends of separate styles previously used by the Byzantines (to transform temples into Christian basilicas) and Arabs (to construct palaces, residences and religious buildings with typically Oriental stylistic characteristics.) Within this sphere we find, in **Palermo**, the majestic **Cathedral**, the churches of the **Martorana** and **San Giovanni degli Eremiti** (which shows marked Arab influence), the **palaces of La Cuba and La Zisa**, and the **Norman Palace** with the **Palatine Chapel**. In the **Palatine Chapel** and in the **Cathedrals of Cefalù** and **Monreale**, the fantastic, glowing tissue of mosaics achieves an incomparable virtuosity of style.

The buildings of the Gothic period in Sicily are principally defensive. It is impossible to count the castles, strongholds and forts on the island. We will mention only the **Castello Ursino** at Catania and the **Castello Maniace** at Syracuse. Catalan influences penetrated from Spain and left an indelible imprint in the Flamboyant Gothic elements commonly found in the decoration of palaces and churches, with a profusion of portals, windows and ornamental features.

At the same time the private building activity of the great noble houses was developing and producing powerful and stylistically perfect fortified dwellings. An outstanding example is the Chiaramonte family, whose influential style, called after them 'Chiaramontana', is embodied in the numerous Steri.

Between the fifteenth and sixteenth centuries Sicily produced, in the genius of the painter Antonello da Messina, one of the most brilliant manifestations of the European painting of the time. Other painters we should mention include the De Salibas and Iacobello da Messina. In the field of sculpture, we have the Renaissance artists of the Gagini family, Domenico, the founder, and his sons Antonello and Antonuzzo. Their unmistakable style can be observed all over Sicily in the decoration of churches and basilicas, in a profusion of figures, arches and finely chiselled bas-reliefs. Another outstanding figure in the sculpture of the period is Francesco Laurana. The Baroque style found in Sicily (seventeenth-eighteenth centuries) one of its most complete expressions, and one with such distinctive features that it is called by the name of Sicilian Baroque. In the context of architec-

The majestic fifth century B.C. doric temple of Segesta.

ture, building activity flourished in different directions; examples are the churches of the Ragusa region, especially the distinctive churches, both dedicated to San Giorgio, built by Gagliardi in Ragusa itself and in Modica, as well as churches in other parts of the island; while Palermo was enhanced by splendid monumental streets and quarters in pure Spanish style. Within the great treasury of Baroque buildings, a distinct strain may be noted at Catania and many minor centres which owe their eighteenth century appearance to massive reconstructions after the earthquake of 1693, largely to be attributed to the architect Vaccarini. In the painting of the time, the influence of the presence in Sicily of famous artists such as Caravaggio and Antonis van Dyck cannot be overlooked. During the nineteenth century the architecture of the island shows the imprint of Neo-Classicism, which left a considerable number of works at Palermo (Orto Botanico and Teatro Massimo), and of Art Nouveau, which was the style of the architect Basile (Villa Igea, Villino Florio).

GEOGRAPHICAL OUTLINE

Morphological descriptions of the Sicilian territory show a prevalence of hilly regions over mountainous or flat regions. In a category by itself is **Mt. Etna**, at 3340 metres the highest peak in the island, the most important active volcano on the Old Continent, and, in spite of its apparent isolation, the true pivot of the contours of the region. The so-called **Sicilian Appenines** are an extension of the Calabrian Appenines and can be divided, from east to west, into the ranges of the **Peloritani**, **Nebrodi-Caroni** and **Madonie**. At about the level of Etna (which, as is well known, stands in the middle of the island), the range of the **Erei** breaks away toward the south-east, while the calcareous plateau of the

5

Iblei, pitted with its characteristic quarries, appears almost cut off from the surrounding territory.

Three great valley systems stand out within the picture of the complex morphology of the island: the **Val di Mazara** to the west, the **Val Demone** to the north and the **Val de Noto** to the south. There are few true plains; we will mention the **Piana di Catania** (the largest), the **Conca d'Oro** (the most famous) and the **Piana di Gela**.

From the point of view of surface water, we have to stress the serious scarcity of water in the region. Efforts have been made to counteract this in recent times by constructing artificial catchment areas and reservoirs (Piana degli Albanesi, Prizzi, Gammauto), while there are many 'bivieri' (bogs) and 'pantani' (marshes) along the coasts. The **Lake of Pergusa**, near Enna, is in fact one of the few examples of natural basins in the island. The most important rivers include the **Salso** (known also as the Imera Meridionale), the **Simeto**, the **Belice**, the **Platani** and the **Gela**. Sicily is surrounded by a series of archipelagoes and small islands, often related to each other by a volcanic matrix. We will mention, proceeding anticlockwise, the Aeolian archipelago (the **Eolie** or Lipari), **Ustica**, the **Egadi** (Aegatian Islands), **Pantelleria**, and the **Pelagie** (Pelagian Islands). There is a strip along the coasts where human intervention has been intense, while the interior, with the exception of a few densely populated centres, suffers from the lack of proper roads and service infrastructures. The characteristics of the Sicilian climate are markedly Mediterranean along the coasts, with mild winters and hot summers, while as we go further inland the factors determining a microclimate of basically continental type become accentuated, so that the winters are colder and the the summers more temperate but with pronounced peaks of heat. The rains are concentrated mostly between Autumn and the beginning of Spring, while a serene sky is one of the outstanding features of the Sicilian climate, which can boast of a very high number of sun-hours during the year.

The colours of the spontaneous vegetation stand out on the eruptive soil of Mount Etna.

PROTECTED AREAS

In the context of environmental protection, Sicily is rapidly falling in line with the decisions of other regions of Italy, respecting what seems to be an inspired international concept for the protection and guardianship of our natural, botanical and zoological heritage.

The **Parco Nazionale dell'Etna** is being set up, while other areas, which in a short time should become the **Parco dei Nebrodi** and the **Parco delle Madonie**, have already been outlined. The Region of Sicily has also passed a law creating numerous protected areas where regulations for the protection of the landscape and natural environment will be applied. Some of the biggest and most important nature reserves are the **Riserva Naturale dei Pantani di Vendicari**, the **Riserva Regionale dell'Isola di Marettimo**, the **Riserva Regionale dello Zingaro**, the **Parco Piano Zucchi**, the **Orto Botanico** and the **Parco della Favorita** and **Parco di Castelnuovo** at Palermo.

BATHS

From the writings of classical Greek authors such as Strabo and Diodorus Siculus, from the many archaeological remains such as the Roman ruins of the Xiphonian Baths *(Acireale)*, from prehistoric vestiges at Termini Imerese and Sciacca and the Roman remains at Terme Vigliatore, the importance of thermal waters in Sicily and their use since immemorial times is immediately clear to us. Baths as an institution and the use of the waters for therapeutic purposes are a tradition many centuries old in Sicily.

Mineral water therapy, inhalation therapy and mud therapy are practised at spas with modern installations. The **Terme Regionali di Acireale** use the waters of St. Venera which are recommended in arthopathy, skin diseases, gynecological problems and diseases of the respiratory tract. The **Terme di Granata Cassibile** (Ali Terme) offer treatment for the sicknesses of childhood, skin diseases, arthropathies, diseases of the respiratory tract and gynecological disorders. The same conditions are treated at the baths of **Germani Marino** (Ali Terme). At the **Terme Gorga** (Calatafimi) sciatica, rheumatism, skin diseases and disorders of the respiratory tract are treated. The **Terme Segestane** (Castellamare del Golfo) are recommended in metabolic disorders, in arthritis in general, in dermatites and disorders of the respiratory tract. At the **Terme di S. Calogero** (Lipari), there are treatments for arthrosis, arthropathies, disorders of the metabolism and obesity. The **Terme Regionali di Sciacca** are recommended for a wide range of treatments, which basically include those so far mentioned. The **Bagni di Sclafani** (Palermo) achieve positive results in the treatment of the after-effects of traumas, in polyarthritis and arthrosis, and in skin and related diseases. The **Fonte di Venere Spa** (Terme Vigliatore) is recommended for liver diseases and disorders of the digestive apparatus and the colon, allergic disorders of the respiratory tract, metabolic disorders, dermatites and arthropathies. The **Terme di Termini Imerese** are helpful in the diseases of childhood, inflammations of the respiratory tract, metabolic disorders and arthropathies in general. At the **Terme di Vulcano** positive results are obtained in the treatment of circulatory disorders, rheumatism, arthropathies, neurites and disorders caused by traumas.

TRADITIONS

In Sicily tradition and folklore are two faces of a reality which we can safely call unique and which manifests itself on the occasion of prevalently religious festivities. It is impossible to count, for example, the celebrations that take place all over the island while the church is commemorating **Holy Week**. Other occasions for folk festivities in the Sicilian calendar are the name-days of the numberless patron saints, historical anniversaries and non-religious festivals.

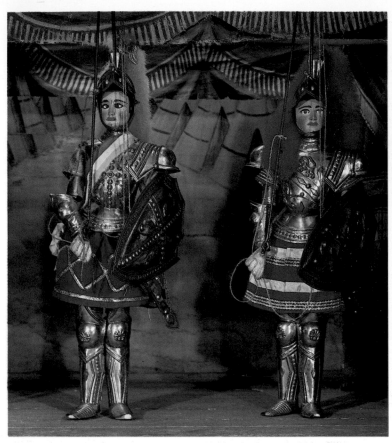

The puppet theatre in the Pitré Ethnographic Museum of Palermo.

In addition to the colourful island costumes, the **Sicilian Cart** is a unique symbolic item, and at the same time, with its rich painted decorations and ornaments, a piece of the history of the island, a natural and genuine expression of its popular culture. So also are the instruments used by the people to make music and accompany an evening's dancing, from the curious 'Jew's harp' (scacciapensieri) to the bagpipes and the tambourine; they are all part of the complex and highly colourful ritual, well typified in the models exhibited in the Pitré Ethnographic Museum in Palermo. Among the traditional art forms, the **Opera dei Pupi** deserves a special mention. Recalling the epic deeds of Orlando and the Paladins, the 'Puppet Opera' is a true theatre of the people, a genuine expression of the culture and history of the island.

Outstanding festivals include the **Epiphany**, celebrated according to the Byzantine and Albanian rites (Mezzojuso, Piana degli Albanesi), the **Festival of St. Sebastian** at Acireale, the spectacular festivals of **St. Agatha**, patron saint of Catania, the **Sagra del Mandorlo in Fiore** at Agrigento, the **Carnival of Acireale**, the **Easter Week** festivities at Caltanissetta, the **Diavolata** e **Angelicata** at Adrano, the Easter celebrations according to the Byzantine rite at Piana degli Albanesi, the **Ballo dei Diavoli** at Prizzi, the **Festival of St. Vitus** at Mascalucia, the **Festival (Fistinu) of St. Rosalia** at Palermo, the **Luminara di Caltagirone** on the occasion of the festival of St. James, the **Palio dei Normanni** at Piazza Armerina, the **Sfilata dei Giganti** at Messina, the **Festival of the Madonna del Ponte** at Caltagirone, the **Procession of St. Lucia** at Syracuse and Belpasso.

FOOD

The variety and complexity of the culinary art in Sicily is the result of thousands of years of history, the amassing over the centuries of innumerable different layers of civilization and culture. While Sicilian cuisine is already rich and elaborate in itself, contributions to it from distant places are not to be neglected. There is, in fact, in almost every dish some ingredient from outside the island; the influences may be Greek, Latin, Arab-Norman, Franco-Hispano-Bourbon.

The ancient Greek roots of this cuisine, celebrated by various authors of the period (Trimalchio of Syracuse, Atheneus, Archestratus of Gela), are revealed in simple, natural foods consisting basically of very fresh fish and natural herbs, since special spices and condiments still had to be imported. The Greek cuisine remained true to itself during the time of the Roman occupation, when the island was the 'granary' of the Empire.

The Arabs were responsible for a distinctive trend which to a great extent is at work still today in the food habits of the people of Sicily. They introduced the custom of using Oriental spices in foods, inventing dishes made of 'flour in the shape of threads' (triyah, or the forerunner of modern vermicelli), teaching Sicilians the very famous cuscus, much used in the Trapani region and at Pantelleria, the typical arancine (a sort of derivative of the Arab pilaf, *using a lot of saffron) and other dishes using rise as a base and adding fish and all kinds of vegetables. Typical foods of Arab origin are* panelle *(a sort of polenta made of fried flour) and the* pasticcio *made of chicken, bread, almonds, pistachios and capers. The influence of Arab civilization can be tasted also in the exquisite concoctions of Sicilian cakes- and pastry-cooking (a treat for the greedy and an irresistible temptation at every corner). The famous* cassata *(from the Arab gas at) and* torrone *(cubayta) are in fact Arab inventions. Refined savourers of seasonal delicacies, the Arabs invented icecream, called 'sorbetto' from the Arab word* 3harbat.

There are endless and surprising combinations, with a decidedly Oriental flavour, using water-melon, pistachio, jasmine (scurzunera), cinnamon, white coffee, almonds.

The Normans, who took over from the Arabs, introduced no substantial changes in culinary habits, which retained their markedly Arab and Oriental character. Game began to be served at this time, while later French influence was responsible for the introduction of the gateau (now more simply called gattò) *made of potatoes and rice, other vegetable dishes and the fish soups (*madelotte*).*

The use of chick peas with pasta, dressed with oil or in other combinations, recalls the events connected with the revolt of the Sicilian Vespers. It is to the Spanish who ruled Sicily from the fifteenth to the eighteenth century that Sicilians owe the introduction of raw materials and condiments from the New World, as well as typically Spanish food customs. With the importation of peppers, tomatoes, aubergines and potatoes, new tastes were added to the cuisine already existing, giving rise to new blends of foods and combining well chosen ingredients, while at the same time Hispanic usages and customs still deeply rooted in the life of the Sicilians were spreading. In the age of the Bourbons it was the turn of the haute cuisine of the nobles and priests, which created its own version of the simple, popular food of the island traditions, while maintaining its ancient splendours.

As well as the dishes already mentioned, the following are typical of Sicilian cuisine: as hors d'oeuvres, stuffed tomatoes, vegetable caponata, stuffed or crushed olives; as first course, pasta with sardines, pasta 'ncasciata, pasta à la Norma, crispeddi, sfincioni. As main and side dishes we should mention swordfish à la ghiotta, aubergines prepared in various ways, sardines a beccafico, broccoli affogati, falsomagro and a great variety of cheeses, from pecorino *to* tuma *to* primosale. *From the vast array of sweets and cakes we will mention cannoli, frutti di Martorana, agnello pasquale, pignolata and a great variety of* granite.

Sicilian wines are of many different kinds and undoubtedly of high quality, pure and strong with a punch in them and often a touch of Marsala *quality. As well as the various types of Marsala, we will mention Bianco di Alcamo, Regaleali, Corvo di Salaparuta, various kinds of Moscato and Passito (Pantelleria), the excellent wines of the Etna district (white, rosé and red), Malvasia delle Lipari, Ambrato di Comiso and Faro di Messina.*

TIMES OF MUSEUMS

Adrano — *Archaeological Museum*, Tues.-Sat. 9 am-1.30 pm, holidays 9 am-12.30 pm.

Agrigento — *Archaeological Museum*, 9 am-2 pm except Monday.

Caltagirone — *Regional Museum of Ceramics*, Tues.-Sat. 9.30 am-2 pm; holidays 9 am-1 pm.

Caltanissetta — *City Museum*, 9 am-1.30 pm except holidays.

Castelvetrano — *Selinunte Museum*, Thurs. 9 am-1 pm.

Catania — *Bellini Museum*, 9 am-1.30 pm; holidays 9 am-1 pm.

Catania — *City Museum*, 9 am-2 pm; holidays 9 am-12.30 pm.

Cefalù — *Mandralisca Museum*, 9.30 am-12 noon, 3.30 pm-6 pm; holidays 9.30 am-12 noon.

Enna — *Alessi Museum*, 9 am-12.30 pm in Summer, Tues., Thurs., Sat..

Erice — *A. Cordici City Museum*, 9 am-2 pm, 3 pm-5 pm; Sat. 9 am-2 pm; holidays 9 am-1 pm.

Gela — *Archaeological Museum*, 9 am-2 pm except Monday.

Lentini — *Archaeological Museum*, 9 am-2 pm except Monday; holidays 9 am-1 pm.

Lipari — *Aeolian Archaeological Museum*, 9 am-2 pm except Monday, holidays 9 am-1 pm.

Marsala — *Lilibeo National Museum*, 9 am-1 pm, 4.30-6.30 pm.

Messina — *Cambria Zoological Museum*, 9 am-12.30 pm (inform in advance).

Messina — *Regional Museum*, 9 am-2 pm; Tues., Thurs., Sat. also 3 pm-6 pm; holidays 9 am-1 pm.

Modica — *Ibla Museum of Popular Arts and Traditions*, 8 am-2 pm except holidays.

Noto — *City Museum*, 9 am-1 pm.

Palermo — *Archaeological Museum*, 9 am-1.30 pm; Tues. and Fri. also 3 pm-6 pm; holidays 9 am-12.30 pm.

Palermo — *E. Restivo Modern Art Gallery*, 9 am-1 pm except Mon.; Tues., Thurs., Sat. also 4.30 pm-7 pm.

Palermo — *International Marionette Museum*, 10 am-1 pm, 5.30 pm-7 pm; holidays 10 am-1 pm.

Palermo — *Mormino Foundation*, 9 am-1 pm, 3 pm-5 pm; Sat. 9 am-1 pm.

Palermo — *Pitré Ethnographic Museum*, 9 am-1 pm except Fri..

Palermo — *Regional Gallery of Sicily*, 9 am-1 pm; Tues., Thurs., Fri. also 3 pm-6 pm; holidays 9 am-12.30 pm.

Palermo — *Risorgimento Museum*, Mon., Wed., Fri. 9 am-1 pm.

Ragusa — *Ibla Archaeological Museum*, 9 am-2 pm except Mon.; holidays 9 am-1 pm.

Syracuse — *Regional Gallery*, 9 am-2 pm except Mon.; holidays 9 am-1 pm.

Syracuse — *Regional Archaeological Museum*, 9 am-2 pm; holidays 9 am-1 pm.

Tindari — *Museum*, 9 am-2 pm except Mon.; holidays 9 am-1 pm.

Trapani — *Pepoli National Museum*, 9 am-2pm; Wed. and Fri. also 3 pm-5.30 pm; holidays 9 am-1 pm except Mon..

PALERMO

Historical Note - A large and important city, Palermo opens like a fan out of its picturesque roadstead; above it stand harsh and powerful hills which descend in steps toward the green Conca d'Oro. In spite of the massive invasion of cement over recent decades, the 'Golden Shell' still offers as a whole a spectacular and evocative landscape. The site where Palermo lies was already settled in prehistoric times, because of its extremely favourable climate and geographical situation. First the Sicanians, then the Cretans and Elymians, founded their colonies beside the bay. The Phoenicians were also strongly attracted to the place, and it became a permanent Phoenician colony in the eighth century B.C. Between the sixth and fourth centuries B.C. a new fortified city grew up around the original nucleus of the *Palaeopolis* and that of the more recently developed *Neapolis*. The Syracusans made several unsuccessful attempts to take the new city at the time of the wars against the Carthaginians. What Dionysius was unable to do, however, was accomplished by Pyrrhus, who occupied the town, though for a short time, in 277 B.C. At the time of the Punic Wars this city, with its highly strategic position in the Mediterranean basin, became one of the principal targets of the Roman drive for supremacy. After a fruitless siege in 258 B.C., the stronghold of the Carthiginians in Sicily was forced to yield to the Romans in 254 B.C.; four years later the Romans resisted Hasdrubal's attempt to reconquer it. The Roman Panormus (placename of Greek derivation meaning All-Harbour, with reference to the size of the harbour), increased in comfort and splendour, as we can see from buildings found near Piazza Vittoria. When Roman power declined, between the sixth and ninth centuries, Palermo fell into the hands of barbarian peoples (Vandals, Ostrogoths), who remained in power there in turn until the Byzantines took over in the first half of the sixth century, to be turned out themselves by the Arabs in 831. The Arab period, during which the population grew parallel to the growth of the city, is one of the golden ages in the history of Palermo. It produced splendid Moorish buildings, whole new quarters of the city, prosperous economic and political developments (the city was the seat of the Arab emirate),and made of Palermo an example for the Mediterranean and a main point of contact in the commerce of the Marine Republics. At the beginning of the eleventh century a combined military invasion by Normans and Pisans undermined the Arab occupation; the Arabs had given way to the Normans of Robert Guiscard and Roger by 1072.

An aerial view of the historical centre.

From that date till the last twenty years of the twelfth century the stage was held by the rise and fall of the Normans, who spread out from Palermo all over Sicily, promoting science, culture and the arts. While Palermo was subject to the feudal order, the Church also developed as an institution, which led to the founding and building of new churches; at the same time the mercantile activity and increasing prestige of the Normans bore fruit in marvels of architecture and art. When the Normans declined it was the turn of the Swabians; Frederick II was a great figure on the stage of history, a ruler who attracted the most talented and innovative men of the time, in spite of the combined opposition to him of nobles and papacy. When Frederick died (1250), the city declined inexorably until finally the capital was transferred to Naples (1266); the Angevins and Aragoneses took their turns as rulers in Palermo, which suffered more and more heavily from the arrogance of feudal power and lost the leadership role that had characterized it in previous centuries of its history. The brief interlude of the Vespers (1282) only consolidated the power of the Aragonese, which was a prelude to the long-lasting dominion of the Spanish in Palermo and on the island. Between the sixteenth and seventeenth centuries, the city changed its face again; new fortifications were built and the layout of the town changed substantially. From the social point of view, the population was sorely tried by a series of natural disasters, such as plague and famine; in 1647 Giuseppe d'Alessi led a fruitless and ill-fated attempt at revolt.

In the first half of the eighteenth century, the Savoys and the Austrians ruled until the advent of Charles III, who built his fortune on the foundation of arrogant abuses of power by clergy and nobility.

In the second half of the eighteenth century the Spanish viceroy Caracciolo carried out a series of reforms of which the most striking was the suppression of the tribunal of the Holy Office. As a result of the French Revolution and widespread unrest in the island, the Bourbon rulers introduced a constitution in 1812; this, however, did not contain the revolutionary unrest and a fertile terrain was prepared for the victorious enterprise of Garibaldi (1860). The city of our days, reborn from the ruins of the Second World War, is one of the principal ports in the Mediterranean, a centre for industry, service industries and crafts, and one of the chief tourist attractions of the south, situated as it is in a context of great historical, artistic and cultural beauty and interest. The most important folk festivals of the city include the celebrations for its patron saint (11th-15th July); the so-called *Fistinu* culminates in the procession with the great car of St. Rosalia, on top of which the coffin with the remains of the saint is borne. The festivities traditionally conclude with a spectacular show of fireworks. Palermo is also one of the towns where we can see the traditional performances of the Teatro dei Pupi (Puppet Theatre). Crafts include pottery of traditional and modern inspiration, refined and decorative majolicas, the figures of the Christmas crib, miniature models of the typical and colourful Sicilian carts (once in common use, but now only 'local colour' for festivals, village fairs and folk spectacles), the traditional puppets, articles in wrought iron and copper, weavings and yarns, the 'palms' used in the Palm Sunday celebrations and the paper flags with the image of Santa Rosalia. The best place to buy traditional goods is around Piazza Vigliena (Quattro Canti), where the most exclusive stores are found, while shops selling goods in the lower price ranges are scattered between Via Maqueda and Via Roma. There exist many traditional markets, such as the Mercato delle Pulci (Flea Market, in Piazza D. Peranni), an interesting display of antiques and other objects of various kinds, the Casa Professa market (Albergheria) for linen and used clothes, the Mercato dei Lattarini (Piazza Borsa), where American goods for camping and life in the open air are sold, the Mercato del Capo (Porta Carini), which sells flowers, vegetables, fruit and clothes, the picturesque Mercato della Vucciria (Piazza Concordia), a big food market reminiscent of the East with an atmosphere of lights, smells, tastes and sounds close to the life of the people, and the market of Piazza Ballarò, traditionally for fruit and fish. We must also remember the great variety of local itinerant markets which can be found almost any day of the week, while the most important local and generally Sicilian craft items can be picked up at the Negozio dell'Artigianato Siciliano run by the various Chambers of Commerce (Via Amari 13), which exhibits an immense choice of merchandise. From the gastronomic point of view, the city is no exception to the traditional rule of Sicilian cuisine; a stop for some of its rich dishes and delicious cakes, sweets and typical icecreams is a must, and greedy tourists can enjoy them in the excellent restaurants and cafés of the capital of Sicily. A last piece of advice that tourists would do well to take seriously concerns the chaotic traffic of this great southern metropolis. On the long

The southern porch of the cathedral, a Catalan-Gothic work from the late fifteenth century.

main arterial roads and in the whole centre, and also in outlying suburbs and the new districts, the traffic is frantic and asphyxiating. For anyone who wants to visit the many historical and artistic monuments of this wonderful city in peace, it is not at all advisable to use a private car, also because it is extremely difficult to find parking places. It is much better to use public transport or the proverbial 'St. Francis' horse' (that is, to walk); this is true also for reaching the zone between Piazza Ruggero Settimo and Piazza Vigliena, where the people of Palermo go to meet each other and have their evening stroll.

Cathedral - This majestic building is imposing for its dramatic outline and the way it rises at the end of the square of the same name (Piazza della Cattedrale), which was built over an ancient cemetery and is surrounded by a marble balustrade with sculptures in Baroque style on it. The appearance of this monumental church is eclectic, since Arab, Norman, Gothic and Baroque architectural elements all coexist in it, but at the same time it is extremely impressive as a whole. It was begun in 1184 by order of Archbishop Gualterio Offamilio, on the site of a previous Muslim building, and is the product of a series of rebuildings, additions and modifications over many centuries. The four bell-towers were built in the fourteenth century; the south and north porches were built in that order between the fifteenth and sixteenth centuries; and in the eighteenth century and beginning of the nineteenth the building was substantially altered by a remodelling in dubious taste by F. Fuga, who changed the plan according to Neo-Classical models and built the dome over the transept.
The *façade* dates from the fourteenth and fifteenth centuries and is framed by two bell-towers adorned with very fine carved motifs recalling

A treasure from the Cathedral: the tiara of Constance II of Aragon from the thirteenth century.

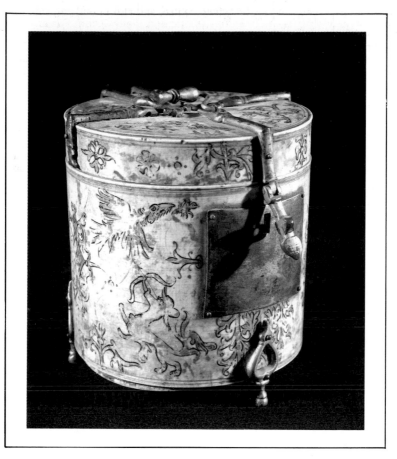

A treasure from the Cathedral: a thirteenth century glass vessel, of Sicilian-Arabic origin.

Islamic decorations in the interweaving of plant and abstract elements. The splendid fifteenth-century portal is rich in decorative details in Gothic style. On the side toward the square is the south porch, a work of Catalan Gothic of great architectural importance (second half of the fifteenth century). The three ogival arches supported by elegant pillars are richly decorated and support a tympanum with fine bas-reliefs. The door under the porch is a fifteenth century work by Gambara. In the same part of the building are monuments, sculptures from the Gagini workshop and plaques commemorating the consecration of the Cathedral. The **apse** between the two towers is the most important portion remaining of the original Norman building. The north porch dates from the sixteenth century, and was decorated by followers of the Gaginis; substantially altered in the eighteenth century, it is still the entrance on the north side of the building and has a seventeenth century door.

The **interior** of the original building was very different from the present one, which is the result of considerable remodelling in the eighteenth century under the direction of F. Fuga. Divided into nave and aisles by a series of pillars, against which stand the Gagini statues of *Saints* (once part of a demolished apse), it is predominantly Neo-Classical in appearance. In the right aisle, in a bay to the left of the entrance from the square, are the *royal and imperial tombs*, to be exact those of Henry VI (+ 1197), Frederick II (+ 1250), the Empress Constance (+1198) and Roger (+1154). Continuing up the right nave, the first chapel, called **Chapel of Madonna della Lettera**, houses a Virgin and Child in Byzantine style. In the **Chapel of San Ignazio** we can see a picture by Novelli: the Virgin with St. Ignatius and St. Francis Xavier. Then comes the **Chapel of the Beato Jeremia**, with the image of St. Jeremiah, and an eighteenth century painting over the altar. In the Chapel of the Relics are the coffin of St. Cristina, from the Gagini workshop, and the coffin of St. Ninfa, the work of Nibilio Gagini. The next chapel, that of San Francesco di Paola, has eighteenth century works by G.B. Ragusa and G. Vitaliano. Then comes the Altar of the Assunta, with an Assumption attributed to G. Velasquez and some remarkable bas-reliefs by Antonello Gagini. On the right side of the presbytery is the **Chapel of Santa Rosalia**, where a bronze railing protects the niche with the silver *urn* containing the mortal remains of the patron saint of the city. The walls are adorned with nineteenth century paintings. The presbytery contains various architectural elements of the original Norman building. We can see the remains of previous structures, while many of the sculptures of the Gagini school also come from the tribune that adorned the apse before it was dismantled during the remodelling. We should notice the Easter candlestick, a valuable Norman work with mosaic decorations, the wooden choir stalls in fifteenth century Catalan-Gothic style and the royal throne. The frescoes in the vault of the choir and apse are from the beginning of the last century.

On the right side of the apse is the entrance to the anteroom of the Sacristy, from which a magnificent fifteenth century portal leads into the **Treasury**, where rich vestments, altar cloths, holy vessels, monstrances, miniatures of the fourteenth to eighteenth centuries and other valuable objects can be seen. Next door, the **Sagrestia dei Canonici** (Sacristy of the Canons) has sixteenth century portals by V. Gagini. In the adjacent **Sagrestia Nuova** (New Sacristy) is a *Virgin* attributed to A. Gagini. In the left transept is the **Chapel of the Sacramento** which houses a precious seventeenth century lapislazuli ciborium, made by an artist from Bergamo and of very striking appearance. On the right is the eighteenth century *mausoleum of the Archbishop Sanseverino*, attributed to G. Pennino. Descending the left aisle we find the Altar of the Crucifix with a sixteenth century wooden Christ and a Madonna and the Magdalene attributed to G. Serpotta; the fine bas-reliefs over the altar by F. and V. Gagini claim our attention. In the next chapel is a fifteenth century sculpture by F. Laurana, the 'Madonna di Libera Inferni'. The following chapel is adorned by a seventeenth century painting of the Martrydom of St. Agatha, by P. Martorana. Two chapels further on, over the altar, is a St. Cristina attributed to G. Velasquez. In the second to last chapel the altar has fine bas-reliefs by the Gaginis. Then comes the baptismal font, the carvings on which represent Adam and Eve and are the work of the Penninos (beginning of the nineteenth century). We should also remark, against the fourth pilaster on the right of the nave, a beautiful sixteenth century holy water stoup, the work of disciples of the Gaginis, and against the pillar opposite (on the left side of the nave) a stoup of uncertain authorship; some scholars, in fact, consider it to be the work of Domenico Gagini, others of Pietro da Bonate.

The **crypt** is later than the original building; it is entered on the left and has two transverse aisles divided by granite columns and a cross vault. It is worth noticing the seven little apses on the side opposite the entrance and the many monuments of archbishops of Palermo, including that of Gualtiero Offamilio, founder of the Cathedral.

Church of Santa Maria dell'Ammiraglio - Known also as *the Martorana*, this church was founded in the first half of the twelfth century by Roger's admiral, George of Antioch. The present appearance of the building is eclectic, combining features of the elevated Norman architectural style and Baroque elements added later. The **façade**, which is obviously Baroque in origin, is from the second half of the sixteenth century. The very fine **Bell tower** has four storeys, lightened by the play of the lancet windows, the slim pillars and the colourful inlays.

The **interior**, also substantially altered by Baroque remodelling, is divided into a nave and two aisles and is particularly memorable for its mosaics. On the right wall, beyond an ancient door, is the mosaic of *Christ crowning Roger II*; on the left wall are a *Madonna of the Rosary* attributed to Zoppo di Gangi and a mosaic representing *George of Antioch at the feet of the Virgin*. The dome, the tambour, the vault and the two small apses are all decorated with beautiful mosaics on religious subjects. In the upper choir (eighteenth century) are many paintings of that date by G. Borremans, who also frescoed the middle portion of the building. The presbytery dates from the seventeenth century; it is dominated by a sixteenth century Ascension by Vincenzo da Pavia and has a precious tabernacle over the altar.

Santa Maria dell'Ammiraglio: the vault with Christ blessing and the four Archangels.

Church of San Cataldo - A strange building of the second half of the twelfth century, this church is in the shape of an oblong block with Arabic crenellations and three small red domes on top. Built in Norman times, it was once the chapel of a palace no longer existing. The **interior**, which has an aisle and naves divided by ancient columns, is very bare yet still possesses a special fascination. It has a fine mosaic floor.

Church of San Giovanni degli Eremiti - This church of the Norman period was built by order of Roger in the first half of the twelfth century, on the site of a previous Gregorian monastery. Considerably remodelled in the second half of the last century, it is a typical example of Muslim architecture and was built by Arab craftsmen who were active at that time in Palermo. The bell tower is a simple, austere structure with lancet windows in its sides; it is crowned by a small red dome which combines with the other domes in the complex to give the whole building a strongly Oriental appearance.

The **interior** is extremely simple and without ornamentation. Two great ogival arches span the single nave, while the transept is divided into three apses of semicircular form. On the right side of the transept is the entrance to some rooms outside the church on the right, which can be identified as the remains of an ancient building of the tenth or eleventh century. It is highly doubtful that they were once part of a mosque. The fine **Cloister** is also Norman (thirteenth century) and is part of an ancient Benedictine monastery. The lovely, lush garden, full of greenery, is surrounded by rows of little ogival arches supported by elegant twin columns.

San Giovanni degli Eremiti: the evocative thirteenth century cloister.
Opposite: the Palatine Chapel, Christ blessing in the central
apse, a Byzantine work from the twelfth century.

Palazzo dei Normanni - This grandly monumental building, known also
as the *Royal Palace*, probably arose on an ancient site in the ninth century, during the Arab period. From the eleventh century, the palace was
the seat of the Norman and Swabian kings. Restored in the sixteenth century, it was from time to time the residence of viceroys and royal per-
sonages of various European houses. Since 1947 it has been the seat of
the *Sicilian Regional Assembly*.
The **façade**, which is of strongly sixteenth century appearance, was
several times remodelled and rebuilt from the seventeenth century on.
On the right stands the **Torre Pisana** (Pisan Tower), also called *Torre
di Santa Ninfa*, which is one of the most easily visible parts of the original
Norman building. By way of an interesting seventeenth century courtyard, with porches and loggias, we come to an imposing staircase leading
up to the first floor, where by far the most interesting portion of the
whole complex is situated.
The **Palatine Chapel** is counted among the finest and most typical examples of Norman art in the Sicilian capital. It was begun in 1130 and
consecrated in 1143. The outer walls of the chapel have been made partly invisible by later construction work;for example the seventeenth century façade has hidden the apse. The **interior** has a nave and aisles divided
by ancient columns sustaining ogival arches; the same architectural traits
find their highest expression in the raised sanctuary, the triple apse and
the dome. The ornamentation of the chapel is marked by the extraordinary quality and beauty of its mosaics, and the very fine wooden *ceiling*
(twelfth century), the work of Fatimite craftsmen. The most important of
the mosaic decorations, carried out by Byzantine artists in the twelfth
century, include the *Christ the Pantocrator with Archangels and Angels*
(in the dome) and the *episodes from the life of Christ* in the apse and
on the walls of the sanctuary. On the left side of the apse is the 'Madonna
Hodigitria', while the walls of the nave represent Bible stories. In the
aisles, the subjects of the mosaics are episodes from the lives of St. Peter
and St. Paul. We observe the beautiful floors, also mosaic, the *ambo*
(twelfth century), and the *Easter candlestick*, which possess fine architectural and sculptural qualities. A small staircase below the ambo leads to
the **Crypt**, where the remains of William I once lay; they were later removed to the Cathedral of Monreale. The *Crucifix* on the wall is from
the sixteenth century. In the **Sacristy** rooms we can see a valuable *Treasury* with vestments and altar cloths, silver vessels, finally worked caskets
in Arab and Byzantine style and parchments.
There are rooms of considerable interest on the second floor of the Palazzo dei Normanni also; we will mention the so-called **Salone d'Ercole**,

Palazzo dei Normanni: two details of the mosaics adorning the "Room of King Roger".

the walls and ceiling of which are decorated with frescoes representing the legends of the mythical Hercules who gave his name to the room, which is now the seat of the deliberations of the Sicilian Regional Assembly. The room was built in the second half of the sixteenth century, and Giuseppe Velasquez painted the frescoes on the walls and ceiling in the eighteenth century. Around the sixteenth century *Cortile della Fontana* (Courtyard of the Fountain) lie the apartments of the 'piano nobile', which have eighteenth and nineteenth century furnishings and decorations. We can visit also the *Room of the Viceroys*, where the portraits of the viceroys are exhibited. Across an atrium dominated by a turreted structure which is part of the Palace, we reach the splendid *Sala di Re Ruggero* (Room of King Roger), magnificently decorated with rich mosaics in Arab style representing hunting scenes.

The *Torre Pisana*, in which an *Astronomical Observatory* is situated, dominates another room which is rather bare in appearance, although a few vestiges still suggest the rich marble and mosaic decorations that once adorned the walls. Restoration work carried out during the seventies of this century permits us to appreciate, from the first floor, the chronology of the various constructions and additions that this part of the building has undergone over the centuries. Among other rooms, we should note the *Sala degli Armigeri* and the *Sala del Tesoro* (Squires' Room and Treasury).

Porta Nuova - This spectacular construction stands at the beginning of Corso Catalafimi and is almost an appendix of the Palazzo dei Normanni. It was begun in the second half of the sixteenth century to commemorate

20

the entry of Charles V to the city, almost fifty years earlier, through a fifteenth century gate that stood there at that time. The Porta Nuova as we see it today is a monumental construction which unites the characteristics of the triumphal arch with marked Renaissance elements. The interesting pyramidal crowning is decorated with majolica figures representing the *eagle*, the symbol of the senate of Palermo.

Palazzo Senatorio - The present seat of city government overlooks the *Piazza Pretoria*, which is enhanced by the fountain of the same name. The building arose in the second half of the fifteenth century, probably on the site of a previous Aragonese palace. Several times altered (sixteenth, seventeenth and nineteenth centuries), it has a sumptuous **façade**; works that stand out are the seventeenth century *statue of St. Rosalia* attributed to Carlo d'Aprile, and the marble *eagle* over the door, the work of Salvatore Valenti, while some inscriptions on plaques commemorate important events in the city's history.

Important art works in the interior include Sozzo's frescoes (sixteenth century) in the **atrium**, the fine Baroque *portal* by Amato (seventeenth century), and a funerary sculpture in marble, probably of the Roman period. We should note, finally, the allegorical sculpture representing the *Genius of Palermo* (first landing on the stairs), and the **Sala delle Lapidi**, **Sala Gialla** and **Sala di Garibaldi** (Plaque Room, Yellow Room and Garibaldi Room). From the balcony of this room, the famous condottiere of the Risorgimento harangued the crowds in Palermo on the 30th of May, 1860.

Fontana Pretoria - Originally designed for the Florentine residence of Don Pietro di Toledo, this fountain was then bought by the Senate of Palermo, which placed it in front of its own building. A spectacular and superb work of the sixteenth century, it was made by the Florentine artists Francesco Cammilliani and Michelangelo Naccerino, who created masterful allegorical, mythological and monstrous sculptures to adorn it. The railing surrounding it is a nineteenth century addition by G.B.F. Basile.

Piazza Pretoria: the monumental fountain adorned with statues by sixteenth century Florentine artists.

Francesco Laurana: the famous bust of Eleanor of Aragon from the fifteenth century. Antonello da Messina: the Virgin of the Annunciation, the masterpiece among the Gallery's paintings.

Regional Gallery of Sicily - The Regional Gallery of Sicily is housed in the fifteenth century Palazzo Abatellis, built in 1490-1495 by Matteo Carnelivari, a fine example of the blending of the Late Gothic and Renaissance architectural styles. This Gallery possesses the most important collection on the island of sculpture and painting, especially of the fourteenth to sixteenth centuries. The sculpture is exhibited on the ground floor, and the painting gallery is on the first floor.

Room I: sixteenth century paintings and wooden sculptures.

Room II: this is the chapel of the palace; it countains some fourteenth and fifteenth century sculptures (particularly interesting is the *sarcophagus of Cecilia Aprile*, attributed to Francesco Laurana) and the impressive fresco of the *Triumph of Death*, of uncertain attribution, perhaps by a collaborator of Pisanello, dating from the mid-fifteenth century.

Room III: various work, outstanding among which is a magnificent Malaga vase with a metallic sheen ("loza dorada") and a Spanish-Arab jar, both from the thirteenth-fourteenth centuries.

Room IV: here we find the very famous *bust of Eleanor of Aragon*, a masterpiece by Francesco Laurana dating from about 1471; it is accompanied by a fine *Portrait of a Gentlewoman*, attribuited to Laurana, and other fifteenth century sculptures of the school of the Gaginis.

Room V: a *Madonna and Child* and a *Portrait of a Girl*, marble statues by Antonello Gagini.

Room VI: more works by the Gagins and by Lombard masters statues by Antonello Gagini.

Room VII and **Room VIII**: paintings of various origins, especially Venetian, Tuscan and Sicilian of the fourteenth and fifteenth centuries.

Room IX: a vast hall in which a series of works by Tommaso de Vigilia, an important late fifteenth century painter from Palermo, stand out.

Room X: this is the room devoted to the *Virgin of the Annunciation*, the great masterpiece of Antonello da Messina, painted around 1473, in which space and light are fused around the figure and face of the Virgin.

Room XI and **XII**: various works by Sicilian masters of the end of the fifteenth century and the beginning of the sixteenth, among which those of Riccardo Quartararo of Sciacca are worth pointing out.

Room XIII: dedicated to Flemish painting: the very famous *Malvagna Triptych* by Jan Gossaert holds the attention.

Rooms XIV, XV and **XVI**: other works by Flemish artists and sixteenth and seventeenth century Italian masters (worth mentioning are Vincenzo da Pavia, Jacopo Palma il Giovane, Mattia Preti).

There is a plan to enlarge the Gallery to include seventeenth and eighteenth century painting, sections for decorative arts, etc.

Regional Archaeological Museum - The museum is housed in the restored *Convent of the Filippini dell'Olivella* and offers us a very interesting collection of Sicilian antiquities in general and of sculptures from Selinunte in particular.

Magna Grecian art: Metope from Selinunte, representing two gods on a chariot, from the sixth century B.C.

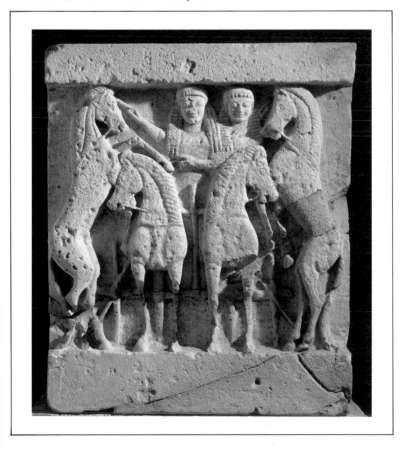

23

Ground floor: We enter through the First Court, where there is a sixteenth century statue of a Triton. In a small room on the right, where objects in Oriental style are kept, are two Sarcophagi in human shape found in the Phoenician burial grounds of Cannita (fifth century B.C.), and an Enthroned divinity with sphinxes, a Phoenician sculpture of a female figure which comes from Solunto (sixth century B.C.).

At the left end on the same side is another small room with Phoenician inscriptions, Egyptian and Punic objects from Motye, and the extremely ancient 'Pietra di Palermo' (Palermo Stone) which is inscribed with a list of the Pharaohs from 3238 to 2990 B.C. In the Large Cloister are sculptures of the Roman period from Tyndaris and Hellenistic finds from Solunto.

In the **Greek Epigraph Room** are interesting inscriptions from Selinunte, such as the Poggioreale Steles (sixth century B.C.), finds from the Sanctuary of the Malophoros and the 'Great Table' of Selinunte. Among other inscriptions we should mention is one from Taormina.

The adjacent **Room of the Bicephalous Selinunte Steles** houses two-headed steles from Selinunte, the work of unknown artists who thus roughly represented their funerary deities (sixth to fourth centuries B.C.). In the **Marconi Room** are architectural fragments and bronze heads found at the Temple of the Victory of Himera (fifth century B.C.). In the **Gabrici Room** we find architectural fragments from Selinunte; this leads into the **Selinunte Room**, which houses the sculptures from the temples of Selinunte. They include, on the right, the Salinas metope (sixth century B.C.), the reliefs representing dancing scenes (second half of the sixth century B.C) and the Rape of Kephalos (fifth century B.C.). On the left side are sculptures, oil-lamps, statues of female figures and reconstructions of parts of temples C and F. The metopes of temple C (sixth century B.C.) represent the Chariot of Apollo, Perseus and the Gorgon, Hercules and the Cercopes. Fragments of metope from temple F (sixth century B.C.) show the Gigantomachia of Dionysius and Athena. Against the back wall are some metopes from temple E (fifth century B.C.), representing Hercules and the Amazon, Hera and Zeus, Artemis and Actaeon, Athena and Enceladus. We should note particularly the hieratic figure of the Ephebus of Selinunte in the centre of the room, a very fine little bronze of the fifth century B.C. There follows a series of small rooms where the Casuccini Collection is displayed; this is a valuable collection of Etruscan art from Chiusi, including finds from the seventh to first century B.C.

First floor: we ascend to the **North Gallery**, where finds from Solunto and the necropolises of Bagheria, Himera and Termini Imerese are displayed. There follow objects found in the area of Segesta (pottery, masks and jewellery), and in the Greek and Roman necropolises of the Lilybaeum region and the burial grounds of Motye.

In the West Gallery are finds from necropolises in the city going back to the Carthagian period, jewels and pottery of Attic and Italiot type.

In the **Terracotta Room** we find antiquities of various origins, mostly terracottas, masks and statuettes, found at Megara, Camarina, Medma, Gela, Centuripe, Agrigentum, Naxos, Tyndaris, Lipari, San Giuseppe Iato, Grammichele.

The Bronze Room displays votive bronzes from Castronovo, materials of Etrusco-Roman origin, a famous bronze from Syracuse, an important example of Greek art from the Castello Maniace, the Ram, and the spout of a fountain from Pompei with a carving of an Athlete killing a stag.

In the **Gallery of Selinunte Terracotta** are many terracotta objects (ex votos) from the Selinunte area, especially from the Sanctuary of the Malophoros (statuettes, masks, busts and pinakes).

The **Sculpture Rooms** house objects of Greek and Roman origin, such as fragments of the Parthenon frieze, Attic reliefs on funerary subjects, Roman copies of Greek originals, the Roman relief with the Sacrifice of Augustus, portraits from Tyndaris and sculptures of Athena and Kore.

Second floor: admirable examples of the prehistoric art of Sicily, from the Palaeolithic to the Bronze Age, are exhibited in the different rooms. They include finds from Levanzo and graffiti from the Addaura cave; the vestiges of the Stentinello culture, found at the village of the same name near Syracuse, are one of the most important discoveries in the history of archaeology in southern Italy. We can also see objects from the Conca d'Oro connected with the Aeneolithic period and Bronze Age finds from the necropolis of Castelluccio and the Petralia Sottana, Partanna, Naro and Sant'Angelo Muxaro sites. The well known tholos tombs come from

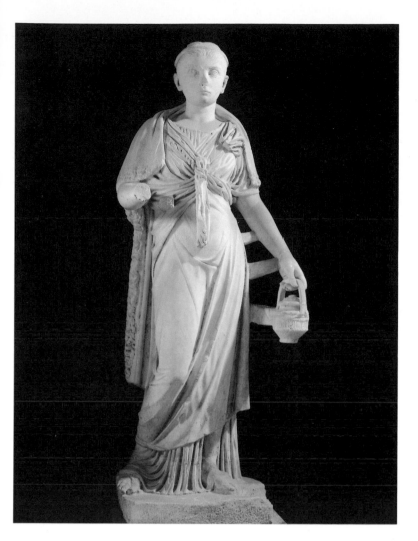

Roman art: priestess of Isis, a work in marble from Taormina (late second century B.C.).

the last named locality; many of the finds date from the Iron Age and were discovered during digs in the eastern part of the island.

The **Greek ceramic collections** include Attic vases with the typical red and black figures, as well as Italiot, proto-Corinthian, Corinthian, Ionian and Laconian works. Among the Italiot vases, which date from the fifth to fourth centuries B.C., we can distinguish those of the Pisticci painter, the Apulian painter of Naples, and the Siceliot painter of Lipari.

In the **Mosaic Room** we find frescoes from Selinunte similar to those of Pompeii and mosaic decorations found at Palermo in the Roman buildings of Piazza Vittoria, dating from the second and third centuries A.D. Worth mentioning are those representing the Seasons, Neptune and Orpheus with the animals.

In the **Himera Room** are finds from the various temples of Himera, including architectural fragments, ornaments, bronze sculptures and terracottas.

Parco della Favorita: Palazzina Cinese.

Palazzina Cinese - In the upper part of the huge park, *Parco della Favorita* (which possesses green space for public use and sports installations), on the slopes of Monte Pellegrino, rises this distinctive small palace built by the architect V. Marvuglia between the end of the eighteenth century and the beginning of the nineteenth centuries. He gave it the combination, typical at that time, of Neo-Classical regularity with a taste for everything exotic and connected with the East. In the rooms, we note the decorations in different styles, furniture of the time and a collection of Chinese and English silks and prints. The frescoes which enhance some of the rooms were painted by V. Riolo, G. Patania and G. Velasquez.

Pitré Ethnographic Museum - This interesting collection was founded by Pitré in 1909 and is housed in a building to the right of the Palazzina Cinese, in the Parco della Favorita.
In *Room I* are furnishings and models of rustic houses.
In *Room II* we can see yarns and weavings with the tools used in making them.
In *Room III* we find interesting costumes of the island.
In *Room IV* are festival costumes, embroidery and ornaments.
In *Room V* is a collection of Christmas costumes.
In *Room VI* hunting implements are displayed.
Room VII focuses on fishing; we find implements, boats and interesting miniatures.
Room VIII accomodates models of ploughs and agricultural implements.
In *Room IX* the implements used in sheep-farming are exhibited.
Rooms X-XI display the tools for itinerant arts, trades and commerce.
In *Rooms XII-XV* we find objects connected with magic and religion, talismans against spells and the evil eye, ex-votos, masks.
Rooms XVI-XVII are laid out to represent a rustic kitchen.
In *Room XVIII* we can see Christmas cribs; there is a particularly interesting eighteenth century one from Trapani.

Room XIX displays costumes, statues and other objects connected with the Easter processions.

In **Room XX** the costumes of the confraternities and some wooden statues are on show.

In **Room XXI** we find articles connected with the chariots of the religious processions; there is a wooden model of the chariot of Santa Rosalia.

In **Room XXII** is a puppet theatre.

Room XXIII displays the decorations of the Sicilian cart and an example of one.

Rooms XXIV-XXVII are decorated as a bourgeois apartment of the seventeenth century.

In **Rooms XXVIII-XXXII** are various objects in terracotta.

Room XXXIII exhibits intaglios and other handicrafts.

In **Room XXXIV** musical instruments are displayed.

On the first floor in **Rooms XXXV-XL** is a well stocked library on subjects of ethnography and Italian and foreign folklore.

In **Room XXXIX** we can see documents with Pitré's signature and many letters.

MONDELLO

A pleasant bathing and residential centre, **Mondello** enjoys a picturesque situation facing the bay between Punta Valdesi and the fishing centre. The town itself is practically part of the capital; long, straight roads join it to Palermo, crossing the beautiful Parco della Favorita or following the coast road below Monte Pellegrino which goes by **Vergine Maria** (on the right, on the slope of the mountain, is the monumental cemetery called *Cimitero dei Rotoli*) and **Arenella**. In the oldest part of the town, where we can see the colourful boats of the fishermen, are two **watch-towers** built in the fifteenth century as part of the coastal defense works. Projecting into the sea in the centre of the bay is the distinctive outline of the **bathing establishment**, built in 1912. To the east of **Valdesi**, on the coast road, we find in the slopes of Mount Pellegrino the **Grotte dell'Addaura** (Addaura Caves), which have provided significant proof of the presence of human beings in the area since prehistoric times, the finds from the caves can be seen in the Archaeological Museum in the capital.

Aerial view of the town.

MONREALE

This picturesque town immediately inland from Palermo spreads over the lower slopes of the hills that rise into the ring of calcareous mountains surrounding the Conca d'Oro. Although the Conca d'Oro itself has become in recent decades nothing more than a configuration of the terrain, because of the inexorable advance of concrete paving and buildings which have reduced to a few gardens and isolated green patches the huge spread of citrus farms that gave it its name, Monreale is still exceptional for its pleasant natural setting, the beauty of its panorama and the splendour of its art treasures. It grew up in Norman times around a Benedictine monastery and became the favourite abode of the Norman kings, who often went hunting there. It is known today for its Cathedral and Cloister, one of the main attractions for visitors to the island, its beautiful surroundings and the distinctive character of its buildings, basically medieval with the addition of houses and other buildings of the Baroque period.

The **Duomo** (Cathedral), counted among the purest manifestations of Norman art in Sicily, was built under the auspices of William II in the second half of the twelfth century. Its most distinctive features are the extremely beautiful mosaics which cover the inside walls, creating a fairy-tale atmosphere, and its graceful architectural forms, which show the Fatimite and Muslim influence common at the time. The upper part of the **façade** is an example of an Arabic recurrent ornamental motif, the interlaced arches, while the porch on the lower part, added in the second half of the eighteenth century, creates a link between two powerful turreted structures. These structures, although the left one remained unfinished, complete the picture of the front of the church, defining it spatially and

The Duomo: mosaics from the central nave depicting episodes from the Old Testament. Opposite, the Christ Pantocrator which completely covers the central apse of the church.

giving a sense of balance to the whole, in spite of the dubiously valid eighteenth century addition. The very beautiful portal is enhanced by a splendid bronze door, the work of Bonanno Pisano, of the second half of the twelfth century. A Gagini portico runs down the left side of the building, where we find the entrance to the church. The door is by **Barisano da Trani** (second half of the twelfth century). The exterior of the apse is finely decorated with lava stone inlays and interlaced arches. The **_interior_** of the basilica is majestic and solemn. The Latin cross of its plan is divided into three lengthwise by ancient columns with marvellously carved capitals which support ogival arches. The upper part of the sanctuary is outstanding for its colours and its decorative and architectural qualities; from the ceiling of the main apse the severe gaze of _Christ the Pantocrator_ reaches into every hidden corner of the building, and gives the impression by a curious optical illusion of looking into the visitor's eyes wherever he is standing. The impressive expanse of mosaics on a gold ground is the fruit of the patient work of Byzantine and Arab craftsmen during the twelfth and thirteenth centuries. Besides the already mentioned figure of Christ the Pantocrator, below which is the _Virgin Enthroned with Saints, Apostles and Angels_, we find, in the nave, Biblical episodes from the Old and New Testament and stories of the Norman kings: above the royal throne is the _Crowning of William II_, and above the archbishop's throne, _William II offering the Church to the Virgin_. The wooden trusses of the ceiling are from the first half of the last century and replace the original ones, ruined by fire. The marble floor, with mosaic decorations, dates in part from the sixteenth century. From the right aisle we enter the **Chapel of San Castrense** (sixteenth century), adorned by a ciborium of the same date and a seventeenth century painting by P.A. Novelli of the saint of the same name. From the end of the right transept we enter the **Chapel of the Benedictines**, which contains admirable marble bas-reliefs by Giovanni Marino and Ignazio Marabitti (_Sarcophagus of F. Testa, Sarcophagus of I. Bonanno, Apotheosis of San Benedetto_). In the right aisle of the transept are the _tombs of William I_

The wonderful twelfth century Benedictine cloister, situated at the side of the Cathedral.

Two details of the artistically decorated columns of the cloister.

and William II, while the altar in the right apse has Baroque traits. In the centre of the apse we find the high altar, designed by Valadier (second half of the eighteenth century). The altar in the left apse is Baroque and has a wooden *Crucifix* above it; there is also a marble reliquiary from the workshop of Gagini, representing the *Pietà*, the *Annunciation and Sts. Peter and Paul*. There follow the altar of *Louis IX* and the sarcophagi of *Margaret, Roger* and *Henry of Navarre*. From the **Chapel of the Crucifix**, on the left side of the apse, we enter the **Treasury**, where precious objects of the Norman and Baroque periods are displayed. At the beginning of the right aisle we find the entrance to the stairs to the **terraces** and the top of the Cathedral, from which we enjoy splendid views of the Cloisters, Monreale and the Conca d'Oro.

The attached **Benedictine Abbey** was built at the same time as the Cathedral and underwent various additions up to at least the end of the fourteenth century. The most interesting part of it is the splendid Cloister, which we enter on the right of the Cathedral (from the front). The elegant rows of twin columns support ogival arches of exquisite Arab workmanship; the whole is enhanced by mosaics and lively capitals carved by Byzantine and Islamic artists. At the end of the cloister, inside a court, is a very fine fountain with Moorish and Hispanic characteristics.

The **Chiesa del Monte** is in Baroque taste; the interior of the church is enlivened by stucco decorations by P. Serpotta.

The **Collegiata**, originally built in the seventeenth century, was remodelled later; good paintings and wooden sculptures are preserved there.

The **Church of San Castrense** is also Baroque and possesses an interesting painting by Novelli and stucco ornaments from the Serpotta workshop.

The small **Church of San Antonio** has a graceful eighteenth century Baroque façade. An admirable view can be enjoyed from the public gardens of the **Belvedere**.

The **Abbey of San Martino delle Scale**, a village which has become a holiday resort on the spurs of the hills above Monreale and the plain of Palermo, dates from the second half of the eighteenth century and was built by Venanzio Marvuglia who enlarged a previously existing Benedictine building erected, according to some sources, by Gregory the Great in the sixth century. In the sixteenth century church we find admirable canvases by Zoppo di Gangi, Filippo Paladino and Pietro Novelli, as well as a fine late sixteenth century wooden choir.

The remains of the ancient town of the Magna Grecia.

SOLUNTO

Solunto is a zone of great archaeological interest on the terrassed slopes of Mount Catalfano, a site of great beauty for its landscapes and views. The first settlements here were very probably Phoenician. Later a Punic stronghold together with nearby Palermo and Motye, it was first conquered by the Syracusans (fourth century B.C.) and then by the Romans (third century B.C.). The place went into a rapid decline and was completely abandoned in the second century B.C. Recent archaeological studies allow us to dismiss the hypothesis that the most ancient nucleus was in fact at the nearby locality called Pizza Cannita. The excavations have brought to light the remains of an ancient settlement of urban character, similar to those of other archaeological zones in the island. They can be defined as late Classical in type, with Hellenistic and Roman additions.

In the *Antiquarium* we can see the finds from the archaeological explorations, Punic steles, local coins, pottery, traces of frescoes, bas-reliefs, statuettes and Greek and Roman capitals.

Along the main street, which is flagged in part, we find houses on various levels, shops and tavernae. The *Gymnasium* is in part the result of reconstruction in the second half of the last century; its name derives from an inscription found there. The building, which seems to have nothing in common with the typical Greek 'gymnasium', is an opulent residence with a peristyle on two floors, decorated with Doric and Ionian colonnades, remains of mosaic paving and paintings dating from the first century A.D.

Among the many houses the *Casa di Leda* is outstanding. It was brought to light in the early sixties of this century, and its name derives from the subjects of some paintings from the first century A.D. found in an inside room. In several rooms there are also very interesting mosaics of the second century A.D.; and we should observe, finally, the complex system of cisterns for supplying water. Other houses are also of great interest; some of them have supplied valuable material for the Archaeological Museum in Palermo, while other items are exhibited in the local Antiquarium. In the public area, where there are several exedras, the ruins of two buildings which very probably formed a Punic Sanctuary, have been found.

It is also worth noting the vestiges of the small *Theatre*, once capable of seating 1200 people, and the nearby *Bouleuterion*, where the meetings of the senate were held.

It is believed that in the highest part of the archaeological area there was an **Acropolis** and together with it the oldest part of the settlement, certainly older than the alterations to the built-up area carried out in the fourth century B.C.; present excavations are bringing to light this older area.

BAGHERIA

This is a densely populated agro-industrial centre on the southern slopes of Mount Catalfano, which here extend to the sea, forming the eastern boundary of the gulf of Palermo. The town, which is situated in an area of large citrus groves, became important in the seventeenth century, when the nobility of Palermo chose to reside there because of the favourable climate. Thus in a brief time many villas and residences were built and the nobles escaped there from the summer heat. The town grew up in the shadow of the house of Branciforti of Butera, and developed considerably between the end of the seventeenth and beginning of the eighteenth centuries, when a number of opulent houses were built.

The **Villa Gravina di Palagonia** is from the first half of the eighteenth century and is marked by an elliptical plan. The façade has classical features, while some of the sculptural decorations are fantastic or monstrous.

The **Villa Gravina di Valguarnera**, which was built in the early eighteenth century, recalls in the rich articulation of its façade and its architectural layout in general the architecture of the Renaissance. The carvings which adorn the façade are the work of Marabitti.

The **Villa Bonanni di Cattolica** is also from the first half of the eighteenth century; its rooms have been used to house a *Gallery of Modern and Contemporary Art* with works by Guttuso, who was born in this town, and other artists of our times.

The **Villa Branciforti di Butera**, built in the second half of the seventeenth century, stands out among the other noble houses.

The **Chiesa Madre** is a Baroque church with a façade of the second half of the eighteenth century.

Villa Palagonia: two strange statues depicting imaginary figures.

CEFALÙ

This charming and graceful little town faces the Tyrrhenian sea from a promontory overhung by a huge, rough outcrop of the mountains. Because of its favourable climate and outstanding natural and artistic features, it is counted among the touristic jewels of the Palermo province. It carries on a flourishing tourist trade, while its other economic activities are fishing and farming. The origins of the place are very ancient, dating perhaps from prehistoric times; there are references around the fourth century B.C. to a *Cephaloedion* allied to the Carthaginians in the war against Syracuse. The placename is obviously connected with the peculiar shape of the rock that gives the town its character. Subjected by the Syracusans, it went through various stages before becoming a satellite of Rome (third century B.C.). In the second half of the ninth century A.D. it gravitated to the Arab emirate of the capital. Taken over by the Normans (eleventh century), the town grew considerably and had many large buildings added to it; it later became a feud of the powerful houses of Chiaramonte and Ventimiglia. In the second half of the last century Cefalù took an active if not very successful part in the revolt against the Bourbons. The magnificent **Cathedral** has the usual structural and architectural characteristics of Norman religious buildings, and is in many ways similar to the Cathedral of Monreale. Begun in the first half of the twelfth century, in the time of Roger II, it took a very long time to build and remained in the end partially unfinished. A flight of steps leads to the parvis which is fenced and adorned with statues. The superb **façade** (thirteenth century) is framed between two powerful towers lightened by rows of lancet windows. Its upper part is adorned with small blind arches and interlaced arches of obviously Muslim descent. The lower portico with its ogival arches is from the second half of the fifteenth century and is attributed to Ambrogio da Como. Other outstanding architectural features of the building include the right side, the powerful transept and the triple apse. The monumental **interior** has the characteristics of a basilica; the nave is divided from the aisles by powerful columns with artistic capitals of Roman and Corinthian type. These support elegant ogival arches which reveal Arab influence. In the left aisle is a sixteenth century *Virgin* by Antonello Gagini, while in the right aisle the *baptismal font* (1100) is of particular interest. The entrance to the transept is through a powerful ogival arcade with colossal columns. The presbytery is raised and glows with the luminous mosaics in Byzantine style that adorn it. The floor is also mosaic; on it stand the royal throne and the bishop's throne, also

A picture of the ancient fishing village and a view from above of the Cathedral.

The apse of the Cathedral with the Byzantine mosaic depicting
Christ the Pantocrator.

enhanced by mosaic inlays. The subjects of the priceless gold-ground mosaics are: in the apse, *Christ the Pantocrator* in the blessing posture surrounded by the *Virgin, Apostles and Archangels*, and on the walls of the tribune, series of *Patriarchs, Prophets and Saints*.

The beautiful adjacent **Cloister** uses very charming architectural elements, especially the rows of small twin columns sustaining graceful ogival arches. We observe particularly the carvings on the capitals, which represent fantastic subjects, mythological figures and fights betwen animals.

The **Osterio Magno** is what is left of a graceful palace of the Norman period, believed to be the residence of **Roger** (twelfth century) although some sources suggest that it was constructed later (fourteenth century). Of particular interest are the fine lancet windows of the old building.

The **Mandralisca Museum** contains valuable paintings of the fifteenth to eighteenth centuries; outstanding in the collection is an admirable work attributed to Antonello da Messina, the *Portrait of an Unknown Man*. There are also fragments of mosaic paving from Roman times, icons in Byzantine style and a large number of finds of archaeological interest from around the town and from Lipari. In particular we should take note of a Greek mosaic of the second to first century B.C, and the Lipari bowl with a picture of a *Seller of Tunny Fish*, an important example of Siceliot pottery of the fourth century B.C. Finally there are Sicilian coins, prehistoric finds, lanterns and other objects of the Greek and Roman ages, vases, clay objects, sulptures, bas-reliefs and Siceliot pottery.

Substantial vestiges remain of the polygonal **walls** of the ancient settlement, dating from the fourth century B.C.

On the rock above the town we can see the remains of a megalithic construction of the fourth to third century B.C., known as the **Temple of Diana**.

The whole coast around Cefalù is dotted with first rank hotels, residences and organized tourist villages.

On the mountain slopes behind the town and reachable by a winding road is the **Sanctuary of Gibilmanna** (seventeenth century), which has a fine altar and a *Virgin* by the Gaginis. The name of the place is of Arab derivation and refers to the presence there of quantities of ash 'manna'.

ISLAND OF USTICA

This island rises from the waters of the Tyrrhenian about 36 miles to the north-west of Palermo and has a wild and fascinating appearance because of the contrast between the intense colours of the sea and the rough volcanic rock formations of its coast (it is geologically similar to Lipari). It is a paradise for lovers of the sea and water sports, and for underwater fishing too, on account of the great variety of its fishes and the rarity of some of them; and is also well equipped with tourist facilities, possessing modern and functional residential complexes. The local economy is strongly supported by fishing and various Mediterranean crops.

The earliest inhabitants there were the Phoenicians; later the Greeks called it *Osteodes*, or the 'ossuary', in memory of the six thousand deported Carthaginians who are traditionally believed to have died of inanition on the island. The Romans gave it the name of *Ustum*, a reference to the blackish, burnt appearance of its volcanic rocks. There was once a Benedictine monastery on the island, around which the first settlement formed; the settlement was several times razed by Saracen pirates. In the second half of the eighteenth century, Ustica was fortified by the Bourbons, which thus allowed organized colonies of settlers from Palermo, Trapani and the Aeolian islands to form.

The coastline of the island is extremely rough and irregular, which creates haunting inlets, sunny coves and rocks towering out of the distant depths of the sea.

The town called Ustica is on the north-east coast and slopes picturesquely down the folds of the **Falconara**, a tufa relief where the remains of an ancient **Necropolis** with underground tombs have been found. An interesting **Museum of Submarine Archaeology** has been set up in the **Torre di Santa Maria**. We can admire there relics of Osteodes, now submerged by the sea, and material from the many wrecks on the sea bottom.

A remote prehistoric settlement dating from the Bronze Age (fourteenth to thirteenth century B.C.) has been identified in the place called **Faraglioni**.

Visitors are recommended to take the trip around the island in a boat, to discover its countless natural beauties, including the many evocative inlets and caves.

Two panoramic views of the island.

TRAPANI

Historical note - The city projects like a wedge into the sea, opposite the Egadi (Aegatian) archipelago and between the slopes of Eryx and the narrow isthmus which overlooks the Lilybaean coast with its extensive salt-flats. An ancient seat of Sicanians and Elymians, it was called *Drepanon* by the Greeks, who were impressed by its sickle form. In the first half of the third century B.C. the city, by then in Punic hands, saw its population considerably increased by the massive migration of people from Eryx ordered by Hamilcar. Long disputed during the Punic wars, it was finally won by the Romans at the naval Battle of the Aegatian Islands (second half of the third century B.C.).

When Roman power declined, various other peoples passed through Trapani, and in the process the city developed a strong business sense. Already important under the Arabs and the Normans, it flourished particularly under the house of Aragon. In the sixteenth century the city was much favoured by Charles V, who also contributed to reinforcing its defense works. In following centuries Trapani further developed its sea trade, its fishing activities and the mining activities connected with the natural abundance of salt in its territory. During the Risorgimento it participated actively in the popular uprisings against the Bourbons. It unfortunately suffered considerable damage during the campaigns of the Second World War, and has today a basically modern appearance, especially on the low coastal land where the urban plan is based on a wide grid. In the peninsular portion, the lay of the land imposes a closer structure, with narrow streets and characteristic alleys.

An important commercial, fishing and tourist port (it is the starting point for trips to the Egadi Islands opposite), it pursues a certain amount of industrial activity, connected with the processing of rural products, salt mining (although this is declining) and fishing. Craft activities include principally coral and mother-of-pearl work (in spite of decreases in recent years), pottery, whistles and marble work. The places where the people of Trapani meet and take their evening walk are concentrated around Via Torrearsa, Corso Vittorio Emmanuele and the panoramic Viale Regina Elena. The Piazza del Mercato del Pesce offers daily the spectacle of fish being sold in a colourful and picturesque setting. In the Rione Palma, every Thursday, the characteristic market of the itinerant vendors is held. In the field of foklore we have the well known *Processione dei Misteri*, which takes place on Good Friday and Easter Saturday. A feature of the procession are the groups of wooden sculptures.

Panorama of the port and the town's sea-front; opposite, some views of the coast where salt is mined.

Sanctuary of the Annunciata - The most important building in the town rises opposite the gardens of Villa Pepoli, almost at the eastern boundary of the built-up area. It was built in the first half of the fourteenth century, but the church as it appears today is the result of almost total remodelling in the second half of the eighteenth century.

The **façade**, adorned with a rose-window and a Gothic portal, is all that is left of the original building; it is flanked by a bell tower of pure Baroque characteristics with a pyramidal crowning. On the left side of the building we find the graceful apse of the Sailors' Chapel.

The **interior**, which has a single nave, has Baroque and Rococo ornamental features. The **Chapel of the Madonna**, which is behind the high altar, is the most artistically significant part of the complex. A sixteenth century bronze railing marks off the marble arch of the same period, richly decorated by the Gaginis. The votive chapel, splendidly enhanced by polychrome marble decorations and roofed by a vault of Arab type, preserves the venerated sculpted image of the **Madonna of Trapani**. This very beautiful sculpture of the *Virgin and Child* is believed to be a fourteenth century work by Nino Pisano or his followers. In an adjacent chapel, decorated with multicoloured marble inlays, is the silver image of *St. Albert*, patron saint of the city. On the left side of the presbytery is the **Sailors' Chapel** (sixteenth century), which has a magnificently ornamented apse. On the right side is the Late Gothic **Fishermen's Chapel** (fifteenth century, frescoed in the following century).

Church of Santa Maria del Gesù - This Renaissance building is interesting for the stone blocks on the façade with gothic features. On the right side is a doorway with a gothic architrave. In the **Staiti Chapel** in the right nave is a highly considered terracotta of a *Madonna of the Angels* by Andrea della Robbia. The marble canopy is attribuited to Antonello Gagini.

Church of Sant'Agostino - This attractive fourteenth century church with clear gothic lines has a typical rose window and a fine doorway. In the little square is a late sixteenth century **Fountain of Saturn**.

ERICE

The classical Eryx, this little town is of great interest to tourists and rises at the top of the mountain of the same name, in a setting with a spectacular landscape and views. It is known that there were already Elymian settlements in the area in the fifth century B.C.; because of its special strategic importance it was the object of recurrent conflicts from ancient times, and in particular of the wars between Greeks and Carthaginians. It was taken by the latter, together with its port of *Drepanon*. Destroyed by the Carthaginians in the first half of the third century B.C., when its inhabitants were transferred to Trapani, it was at the centre of constant fighting with the Romans, who held it after 241 B.C. In Roman times the place was much visited because the celebrated Sanctuary of the Venus of Eryx was there. In medieval times it belonged first to the Arabs and then the Normans, and was called *Monte San Giuliano*.

The fame of the place is connected also with the *Centro Internazionale di Cultura Scientifica 'Ettore Majorana'* (Ettore Majorana International Centre for Scientific Culture), founded there in the sixties. Speaking of folklore, the best known event is the *Processione dei Misteri*, held on Good Friday. Typical craft products are the pottery, the *frazzate* (carpets) and the bags.

The **Chiesa Matrice** is a church of fourteenth century origin; beside it is a powerful battlemented tower pierced by lancet windows. In front of the church, which has a fine rose-window in the middle of the façade, is an ogival-arched porch with Gothic features, added in the fifteenth century, under which we come to the very fine Gothic portal. The interior, which has an aisled nave, is the product of rebuilding in Neo-Gothic style during the last century. In the right aisle, on the third altar, is a *Virgin* believed to be the work of Laurana (fifteenth century). In the left aisle we find fifteenth and sixteenth century chapels. The sixteenth century marble altarpiece in the presbytery is by G. Mancino.

The Chiesa Matrice, fourteenth century.

Some details of the ancient town.

The **Church of San Giovanni Battista** is a building of the Norman Gothic period, and preserves the original door from that time (thirteenth century). Largely remodelled in the seventeenth century, it possesses important sculptures, the most interesting of which are a *St. John the Evangelist* by Antonello Gagini and a *Baptist* by Antonio Gagini.

The **city walls** date from various periods. There is little left of the megalithic walls of the sixth century B.C.; they were mostly rebuilt in the Roman and Norman periods.

Inside the so-called **Castello di Venere** (Castle of Venus), a Norman construction of the twelfth to thirteenth centuries, the few remaining vestiges of the **Temple of Venus** at Eryx have been found. From the crest of the precipitous rock we can admire a splendid panorama sweeping from the Cape of San Vito to Trapani below with the Egadi islands as a background, to the salt-works and Lilybaean coast toward Marsala, and to Valderice. On especially clear days it is possible to make out the coast of Tunisia.

The Pepoli Castle is surrounded by the magnificent garden called **Giardino del Balio**, and is built on the site of the ancient acropolis of Eryx.

The **'A. Cordici' City Museum** is in the Municipal Palace. Its collections consist of archaeological remains from prehistoric to Roman times (there is an important *Head of Aphrodite* of the fifth to fourth centuries B.C.) and paintings from the seventeenth to nineteenth centuries. There is, finally, an interesting collection of coins, and a marble *Annunciation* attributed to Antonello Gagini (first half of the sixteenth century).

41

CASTELLAMMARE DEL GOLFO

A pretty bathing centre in the middle of the gulf of the same name, with a distinctive setting and views. In ancient times it was probably Segesta's outlet to the sea; in the Middle Ages it belonged to Alcamo and was known as *Porto d'Alcamo*.

The **Castle**, built in the fourteenth century, was considerably altered at a later date.

Nearby, at **Terme Segestane**, is a hot salt and sulphur spring, of which the mud and vapours are also used, and which is particularly recommended for arthropathies, arthritis and neuritis, rheumatism, skin complaints, metabolic diseases and problems of the respiratory tract.

West of Castellamare, along the picturesque coast of **Scopello**, we see the imposing shapes of the **Faraglioni** rocks rise from the sea, creating an exceptionally striking landscape.

ALCAMO

This town, known as the birthplace of the thirteenth century poet Ciullo (or Cielo) d'Alcamo, lies in a magnificent setting on the slopes of Mount Bonifato, with a scenic view of the Gulf of Castellamare. The town derives its name from the Arab 'Alqamah who founded it in the ninth century. In the Swabian period (thirteenth century) a new centre was formed lower down, at the foot of Mount Bonifato. From the following century on it was an Aragonese dominion, and later a feud of various noble houses.

The **Chiesa Matrice** is a seventeenth century church named after the Virgin of the Assumption. On the same site previously was a fourteenth century church, of which the portal and the elegant bell tower remain. The interior has an aisled nave and frescoes by Borremans in the apse and dome; It also contains works by Antonio Gagini, such as the *Death of the Virgin* (left aisle) and the *Crucifix* (right aisle), and others by his pupils.

In the seventeenth century **Church of San Francesco** are a marble altarpiece, considered probably to be the work of Domenico Gagini, and two sculptures, representing the *Magdalen* and *St. Mark*, attributed to Antonello Gagini.

The **Badia Nuova**, known also as the *Church of San Francesco di Paola* preserves a painting by P. Novelli and allegorical decorations by G. Serpotta.

In the **Church of San Salvatore** (*Badia Grande*) are other canvases by Novelli and sculptures by Antonio Gagini. The **Church of Sant'Oliva** (eighteenth century) has a painting by Novelli (high altar) and works by the Gaginis, including a figure of Saint Olive, attributed to Antonello.

The **Church of the Santi Paolo e Bartolomeo**, which has characteristically Baroque traits, houses an admirable *Madonna del Miele* (Madonna of the Honey), by an unknown fourteenth century artist.

The **Castle** (fourteenth century) goes back to the Aragonese period, and is square in plan with massive towers at the angles.

CALATAFIMI

This large country town in the upper Val di Mazara was founded before the Roman conquest, and developed during the Arab period around a fortress which gave its name to the locality. A feudal possession during the Middle Ages, it became famous during Garibaldi's Sicilian campaign, when an epic battle, decisive for the capture of Palermo, took place there (15th May 1860). The remains of the **Castle** (thirteenth century) are interesting, as are some Baroque churches. An **Ossuary Monument** recalls the battle between Garibaldi and the Bourbons.

But the most important sight-seeing place in this area is undoubtedly ancient **Segesta**.

Panoramic view of Castellammare del Golfo; the Castle and the Chiesa Matrice at Alcamo; a view from above of Calatafimi.

SEGESTA

This city, founded by the Elymians, was in perpetual conflict with Selinunte and was called by the Greek peoples Egesta. As an ally of the Carthiginians, it was besieged by the Syracusans who captured it toward the end of the fourth century B.C. After various vicissitudes it yielded to Rome (first half of the third century B.C.). The ancient city rose on the terraced slopes of Mount Barbaro and seems to have been gradually abandoned after the Roman conquest, being finally destroyed by the Vandals.

The *Temple* is one of the most significant examples extant of Doric architecture. Dating from the second half of the fifth century B.C., it rises outside the urban area, on a slope on the west side of Mount Barbaro. The temple building is among the best conserved in Italy. The Doric peristyle, never in fact completed, consists of robust archaic columns on

The spectacular fifth century B.C. doric temple.

A partial view of the temple.

a base with three high steps, supporting the powerful entablature; there are tympana in the frontons.

The **Theatre** rises in an evocative setting with an impressive view. Partly built into the hillside, it dates from the fourth to third centuries B.C. and has an auditorium of 20 levels of steps divided into seven blocks. Little is left of the stage, the walls of which were decorated with scenes connected with the god Pan.

In **Contrada Mango** have been found the substantial remains of an Elymian **Sanctuary** of the sixth to fifth century B.C.; some archaeological material has also been found here (pottery, inscriptions and graffiti), but is difficult to decipher and interpret.

An evocative picture of the fourth-third century B.C. theatre.

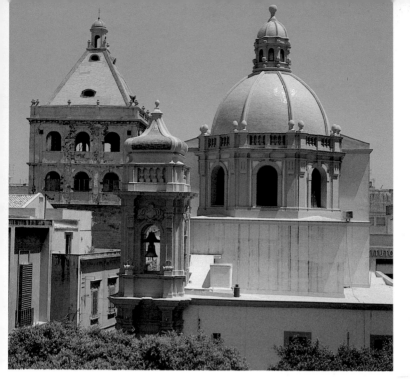

The dome of the Church of San Giuseppe.

MARSALA

Marsala is the town with the largest population in the province of Trapani. It lies on Cape Boeo, otherwise known as *Cape Lilybaeum*, at the westernmost tip of Sicily. The economy of the place is based mostly on wine-growing (strong, sweet Marsala wines are famous), commerce and a certain amount of industry. The place where the present town stands was probably a Sicanian site.

At the beginning of the fourth century B.C. the Carthaginian *Lilybaeum* took the place of nearby Motye. Later a Roman possession and flourishing in the Middle Ages, the town derived its name from the Arab words *Marsa'Ali* (port of Ali). Taken over by the Normans in the twelfth century, it later passed to the House of Aragon; in the sixteenth century the importance of Marsala declined considerably as a consequence of the artificial earthing up of its port, which was done to defend the city against the constant attacks of pirates.

Marsala and its commerce returned to their old splendour in the eighteenth century, when the English promoted activities and trade connected with wine production. The legendary "Landing of the Thousand" on the 11th May 1860 took place at Marsala. In May the town is the scene of the Fiera del Vino dei Paesi Mediterranei (Mediterranean Countries Wine Fair). Visits to wine-cellars and producers are enjoyed by tourists.

The ***Palazzo Comunale***, known also as the *Loggia*, is an elegant eighteenth century building; its façade is marked by the combination of the colonnaded portico on the upper storey and the arcade on the ground floor. In the centre of the façade rises a clock-tower.

The ***Duomo*** (Cathedral) is a seventeenth to eighteenth century building with an unfinished façade. The interior has an aisled nave and possesses various works from the workshop of the Gaginis. We should notice particularly a marble altarpiece in the chapel to the left of the presbytery attributed to Antonello Gagini. In the right transept we can see a fine painting by Riccio (end of the sixteenth century). In a room annexed to the church and arranged as a museum are eight valuable Flemish tapestries (sixteenth century) commissioned by Philip II.

Insula Romana: detail of a third century B.C. mosaic.

The **Lilibeo National Museum** has been set up in the Baglio Anselmi, formerly a wine factory. We can see there archaeologically valuable prehistoric materials, ancient tomb furniture, finds from Motye (especially important is the statue of a man, an original Greek marble from the fifth century B.C.), fragments from Roman times, mosaic decorations and Medieval objects. Among the marine archaeological material, the reconstruction of a Carthaginian liburna (third century B.C.) found in the late sixties, is especially interesting.

The small **Church of San Giovanni** rises on the site of an Early Christian baptistery, believed to have been where the Sibyl of Lilybaeum lived. It is possible to visit the grotto below, where there is a well and a Roman mosaic.

The so-called **Insula Romana** is an area of great archaeological interest which has given up vestiges of the Roman period connected with vast rooms of the third century B.C. with abundant mosaic decorations and the remains of a small bath building. In this area and elsewhere the remains of original Carthaginian and Roman buildings have been excavated.

To the north-east of Marsala, on the **Island of San Pantaleo**, in the so-called *Stagnone*, are the ruins of the town now called Mozia. Ancient **Motye** was, with Palermo and Solunto, one of the main outposts of Phoenician colonization in Sicily (eighth century B.C.). Later a Punic city of considerable importance, it was razed by the Syracusans at the beginning of the fourth century B.C. The most noteworthy ruins are those of the **city wall**, which date from the sixth to fifth centuries B.C., those of a vast burial ground, and a Sanctuary (in the locality of Cappiddazzu) which has provided valuable archaeological information. Also interesting are the remains of a **military dock** from Carthaginian times, and the **Casa dei Mosaici**, a beautiful fourth century B.C. residence with fine mosaics representing animals.

In the **Whitaker Museum** are interesting archaeological finds from mainland Motye and the Lilybaean area in general. We are struck particularly by the Motye Charioteer, a fine sculpture of the school of Selinunte, the tomb furniture and other finds from the Sanctuary and the sacred enclosure where sacrifices were made.

MAZARA DEL VALLO

This small town looks on to the canal-harbour at the mouth of the Mazaro river. A flourishing wine-producing and fishing centre, it is one of the most active maritime and fishing ports in western Sicily. An ancient Phoenician harbour, it belonged for a long time to the sphere of Selinunte, until the arrival of the Carthaginians (fifth century B.C.) and, later, the Roman colonists. In the Middle Ages it was known as *Selinuntina* and became a flourishing centre under the Arabs and Normans. It was in fact the administrative centre for the whole Val di Mazara, losing its prominence only at the beginning of last century, in favour of Trapani. At the end of August the traditional Sagra di San Vito (St. Vitus' Fair) is held there, followed by a historical procession.

The present appearance of the ***Cathedral*** (eleventh century) is the result of rebuilding in the late seventeenth century. In the façade, which has a powerful bell tower beside it, is the portal with the figure in relief of Count Roger on horseback (sixteenth century). The interior, which has an aisled nave, is rich in sculptural decorations: to be noted is the *Transfiguration* by Antonino Gagini in the apse, with ornaments and stuccoes by Ferraro. In the left transept is a *Christ Derided* by Marabitti and a statue of *St. Vincent*, the work of Antonello Gagini. There is also a fine marble portal by Berrettaro (sixteenth century) in the right aisle, and sarcophagi from the Roman period and from the fifteenth and sixteenth centuries, one of them by D. Gagini.

The ***Church of Santa Caterina***, behind the Cathedral, has a statue of St. Catherine by Antonello Gagini.

In the central ***Piazza della Repubblica***, which is enhanced by the façades of eighteenth century buildings, stands a *Statue of San Vito* in Baroque style by I. Marabitti (second half of the eighteenth century).

San Nicolò Regale is a small church whose origins go back to the Norman period (twelfth century). The unusual square structure is topped by

Piazza della Repubblica: in the centre the statue of San Vito by I. Marabitti (second half of the eighteenth century).

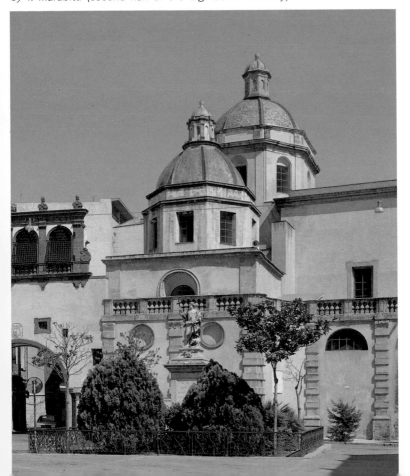

battlements. The interior has an aisled nave and three apses. A late Imperial mosaic floor is preserved in a building opposite the church.

The **Church of San Michele** (seventeenth century) contains admirable sculptures by the circle of the Gaginis and the followers of Serpotta.

The **City Museum**, recently set up in the Jesuit College (seventeenth century), exhibits material of archaeological interest from the Roman period from the area of Mazara, as well as a collection of paintings.

Buildings worth noting include the **Palace of the Knights of Malta** (seventeenth century), the Baroque **Church of Santa Veneranda** and the **Casa Scuderi**, originally built in the fifteenth century and still preserving parts of the ancient structure.

The port and sea-front of the little town.

On the following pages: some views of temple E and temple C,
from respectively the fifth and sixth centuries B.C.

SELINUNTE

The recently founded Archaeological Park of Selinunte takes in a large
part of the area of the municipality of Castelvetrano; the ruins of the ancient city of Selinunte are scattered between the Gaggera hill to the west
and the so-called Collina Orientale (Eastern hill) to the east.

The original settlement was founded in the seventh century B.C. near the
river Selinos (the present Modione), which gave its name to the new colony, founded by people from Megara Hyblaea. The city was in constant
conflict with the Elymians who had one of their most important settlements at Segesta, and for a long time was at enmity with Carthage also.
The Carthaginians, coming to the aid of the people of Segesta, laid siege
to Selinunte (409 B.C.); the town was wrecked, a large number of its inhabitants were massacred, at least 5000 people from Selinunte were
taken captive and the temples were left in ruins. Hermocrates of Syracuse
tried in vain to reorganize the ancient city, which was abandoned in
favour of the Acropolis, and thus spent the dark years of the Phoenician
occupation, until it was completely destroyed by what was left of its own
population to prevent it being conquered by Rome (241 B.C.). A devastating earthquake in the early Middle Ages completed the work of destruction, doing further serious harm to the marvellous ancient buildings,
which have since then been more and more exposed to deterioration and
decay. During the obscure medieval period, even the memory of the ancient Greek city was lost; in Arab times it was known as *Casale degli
Idoli*, and was rediscovered only in the second half of the sixteenth century, by Fasello. The first excavations were begun in the first half of last
century, and provision has been made only in recent times for the definitive disposition of the very interesting archaeological area; the Park was
founded and the Antiquarium set up (it is still being arranged).

On the **Acropolis** we find substantial vestiges of the **ring walls**, rebuilt
under the Phoenicians, and the remains of the powerful fortifications for
which Hermocrates was responsible. Further down we find the remains
of a **sacred enclosure** and **houses** going back to Punic times.

The temples of Selinunte are identified by letters of the alphabet, since
it has not yet been possible to decipher what divinities they were consecrated to.

There is little left of **Temple O**, originally a Doric peripteral temple
which must have had six columns on its façade and fourteen on its sides.
To the north of this are the remains of another Doric peripteral temple,

similar to the first but in a better state of repair. It is known as **Temple A**, and its altar has been found. Both these temples seem to date from the first half of the fifth century B.C. In this zone we see also the remains of a porticoed peripteral building of the same age as the temples, which must have served as a monumental entrance porch.

On the other side of the road which cuts across the Acropolis rise the ruins of **Temple B**, a small building perhaps dedicated to the cult of Aesculapius. It has four columns across its façade, and can be dated to the third to second centuries B.C. because the overlapping of Doric and Ionic styles that we observe in it is characteristic of the architecture of that period.

Nearby rise the colossal ruins of **Temple C**, the most ancient and grandest of the temples of Selinunte. It was founded in the first half of the sixth century B.C., and is a peripteral structure with six frontal columns, and with some of its columns and part of its entablature restored to their places in relatively recent times. In the metopes of the cella, which has a row of four columns in front, were true masterpieces of the sculptor's art; some of them can be seen at the Archaeological Museum in Palermo, where some other ornaments and clay fragments from the same temple are also kept.

The ruins of the Acropolis.

The remains of temple G.

Nearby is what is left of **Temple D**, a Doric peripteral temple originally consisting of six columns across and thirteen on the sides, which was built in the second half of the sixth century B.C. The rest of the Acropolis, where we can see the remains of **houses** of the Punic period and **shops** and commercial zones, also possesses vestiges of **minor temples**, which have given up important archaeological finds, such as the *Salinas Metope*, preserved in the Palermo museum.

At the top edge of the Acropolis, in the middle of some fortified structures of the Carthaginian period, is the **Northern Gate**. On the Eastern hill, perfectly aligned, are temples E, F and G.

Temple G, the northernmost of the three, was certainly the most monumental and vast. It was begun in the second half of the sixth century B.C., but the Carthaginians destroyed the city before it could be finished. Although it is reduced today to a colossal heap of ruins, it has still been possible to reconstruct its plan exactly, and thus to conclude that it was one of the finest examples of Greek temple architecture. It was originally a pseudoperipteral structure with eight columns in front and seventeen on its long sides; inside was a cella, separated off by a double colonnade with ten columns each side and a pronaos with four columns in front. Theories as to the divinity possibly worshipped there are limited to Apollo and Olympian Zeus.

Temple F, the smallest of the three, dates from the middle of the sixth century B.C. and is surrounded by a peristyle with six columns at the ends and fourteen on each side. Inside was the cella with the pronaos and a further enclosed space. Of the many clay decorations that adorned the temple, only two metopes representing mythological motifs remain.

Further down the hill rises **Temple E**, the present appearance of which is the product of recent restoration, making very questionable use of modern building techniques. The original building was a Doric peripteral temple, with six columns in front and fifteen on the sides. It was built

A view of the ruins of the Acropolis.

in the first half of the fifth century B.C., very probably on the site of an even more ancient construction. The cella, which is preceded by a pronaos, was decorated with metopes with mythological scenes, some of which are now on show in the Archaeological Museum in Palermo. Some interpretations suggest that the temple was consecrated to the cult of Hera.

On the Gaggera hill are the remains of the so-called **Sanctuary of the Malophoros**, one of the most famous and oldest sanctuaries of ancient Sicily, which seems to have been erected between the seventh and sixth centuries B.C. Its strange name refers to the cult of Demeter, the 'pomegranate-bearer', which was perhaps practised there. The ruins of the building stand inside a walled zone which enclosed the remains of various sacred areas.

To the north of this are the **Sanctuary of Zeus Meilichios** (the remains of a square enclosure) and **Temple M**, a rectangular structure of the sixth century B.C., probably a monumental fountain.

EGADI ISLANDS

This group of islands off the coast of Trapani has a common origin and geological affinities with Sicily, even if it resembles nearby Africa in climate and landscape. The archipelago, which has recently been equipped with excellent tourist facilities, hotel complexes and organized residences, consists of the islands of Favignana, Levanzo and Marettimo, and the rocks *Formica* and *Maraone*.

The first human settlements there go back to prehistoric times, when the islands were still joined to the coast of Trapani; archaeological findings show that human beings lived there already in Palaeolithic and Neolithic times. In ancient classical times the islands were called *Aegates*; during the Punic Wars they were the scene of the famous naval Battle of the Aegatian Islands where the Roman fleet defeated the Carthaginians (243 B.C.). From then on, being situated on several important trade routes, they became a port of call for Phoenicians, Byzantines and Arabs. Several times subjected to raids by barbarians and pirates, they acquired a relative tranquillity with the arrival of the Normans, only to suffer again from pirate incursions all through the Middle Ages.

The economy of the archipelago is based largely on tourism, owing also to the progressive decline of activities connected with tunny fishing, which for centuries was the main source of wealth, especially for a period beginning in the seventeenth century, when the Egadi Islands were for a long time a mainstay of Genoese economic interests. In the month of May, at the time of the Sagra del Tonno (Tunny Fish Fair), the characteristic and savage rites of the "mattanza" (killing) are revived, attracting swarms of visitors and tourists.

A panoramic view of the sea-front at Levanzo.

Favignana is the largest of the islands, and is situated in the lower part of the archipelago. The ancient *Aegusa* of the Romans, it has provided interesting archaeological information on the periods from prehistory up to the Punic age. The town of Favignana lies on the northern coast, on the slopes of Mount Santa Caterina, the highest rise in the island (314 meters). The little fishing port is an enchanting sight. The Church has the typical characteristics of Sicilian Baroque. The Palazzo Florio is the work of Damiani Almejda, and is a fine example of the work of these well known architects in the second half of last century. Visitors will do well to make the trip around the island in a boat, in order to admire the beauty of its coasts with their caves and many inlets. At Favignana are two important tourist villages, much visited in season.

Levanzo rises from the sea to the north of Favignana, opposite Trapani, and is the nearest to Sicily of the Egadi Islands. Its highest point is the Pizzo del Monaco (278 meters), while the town of Levanzo, which is also the harbour, is on the southern coast. The island, called *Phorbantia* by the Romans, is known for its important vestiges of the Palaeolithic and Neolithic ages. Engravings dating from ten thousand years before the birth of Christ, as well as paintings from five thousand years before Christ, were found in the cave called Grotta del Genoese in the fifties.

Marettimo is the furthest from the mainland of the islands of the archipelago and is also the highest; the Pizzo Falcone, in fact, attains 884 metres. Already known in ancient times as *Hiera*, it was for a long time in the possession of the Arabs, traces of whose influence remain in eating habits (an example is cuscus, the royal dish of Trapani), in dialect expressions and in the style of some buildings. The island has a very evocative natural setting and views, and is one of Sicily's underwater fishing paradises.

Along the picturesque coast we find splendid caves: **Grotta del Cammello**, **Grotta della Bombarda** and **Grotta del Presepio**. The **Cala Mantione** is counted amongst the most picturesque places in the whole archipelago.

ISLAND OF PANTELLERIA

This island, the farthest out tip of Sicilian territory, is only 70 kilometres away from the coast of Tunisia. Already inhabited in the Neolithic period, it was conquered around the seventh century B.C. by the Phoenicians, who called it *Hirani*. Later disputed between Romans and Carthaginians, at the time of the Punic wars, it was won by the former, who changed its name to *Cossyra*. When Rome declined, it was the turn of the Vandals and the Byzantines, until the Arabs arrived. The Arab colonization left its mark in placenames and in the architectural styles still in use today. The island, which was called by the Arabs *Bent el Rion*, was conquered by the Normans in the twelfth century. During the last World War it suffered violent bombing by the Allies.

The island is obviously of volcanic origin, and has the typical characteristics of secondary vulcanism. It is 836 metres high at the volcanic cone of Montagna Grande; and many other small craters can be seen, known locally as *cuddie*. Capers, zibibbo grapes (the Pantelleria 'passito', wine made from dried grapes, is famous) and a growing tourist trade are the main items in the island's economy. Picturesque coasts, evocative inlets and natural caverns are the main attractions of this inviting island, where life goes on according to the rhythms of Mediterranean peasant culture, far from the hectic stress of modern daily life. The clear waters create a paradise for lovers of the sea and underwater fishing.

The most important places for sight-seers include the remains of a prehistoric settlement of the Neolithic period at *Mursia*, not far to the south of Pantelleria, which is the main town on the island, and grew up around the ancient **Barbacane Castle**, rebuilt in the eighteenth century. In the same area we can observe the distinctive **Sesi**, low round towers typical of megalithic funerary architecture.

Amongst the architectural curiosities of the place we must point out also the houses called dammusi, built of stone with vaulted rooves. It is particularly enjoyable to make a tour of the island, either on the coastal road or by boat, in order to appreciate more fully its beautiful landscapes and fine views.

AGRIGENTO

Historical Note - The city rises on the slopes of a mountain plateau bounded by the basins of the Sant'Anna river (the ancient *Hypsas*) and the San Biagio river (the ancient *Akragas*), in an evocative natural setting overlooking the panoramic Valley of the Temples and with the southern coast of the island visible in the distance. It is believed to have been founded by colonists coming from the Greek islands under an understanding with the inhabitants of nearby Gela (sixth century B.C.) In a short time *Akragas* grew in riches and power; under the tyrant Theron it won a battle at Himera (fifth century B.C.) against a much larger Carthaginian

Panorama of the town from the Valley of the Temples.

army. The Carthaginians had their revenge toward the end of the century; the city gave in to hunger after a long siege, and was taken and laid waste. Rebuilt and repopulated by Timoleon, it was a bone of contention between Romans and Carthaginians until the former took firm possession of it, in 210 B.C.

Under Roman protection *Agrigentum* enjoyed a period of calm and active prosperity. Relentless decadence set in under the Byzantines. Having become an Arab possession in the first half of the ninth century, it changed its name to *Girgenti*, which it retained until June 1927 when its present name was introduced.

In the Swabian period it followed the fortunes of Palermo; in the fourteenth century it was subjected by the powerful house of Chiaramonte, from which it got free only toward the end of the century. Under the Aragonese it enjoyed customs exemptions which favoured its already prosperous commercial development. In the second half of the nineteenth century, its inhabitants distinguished themselves in the struggle for freedom from the Bourbon yoke.

Outstanding people who were born at Agrigento include the philosopher Empedocles (fifth century B.C.) and the playwright Luigi Pirandello (1867-1936). With its favourable climate, mild even at the height of the cold season, and its exceptionally fine natural setting and views, it is one of the most popular tourist resorts in Sicily, an internationally celebrated archaeological, architectural and artistic centre.

In early Spring the spectacular blossoming of the almond trees clothes the Valley of the Temples in a veil of strange and evocative beauty, and is the inspiration for the *Sagra del Mandorlo in Fiore* (Fair of the Almond in Flower), which is celebrated with a colourful array of local costumes and folklore and attracts enthusiastic crowds of Italian and especially foreign tourists. Among other festivities are further religious celebrations and the Pirandello festival in the Summer.

The Via Atenea is the hub of the life of the town, the place where the people of Agrigento meet and prefer to stroll at sunset.

Among the most characteristic craft articles on sale we find the 'scacciapensieri' (Jew's harp), the typically Sicilian musical instrument played with the mouth, called locally *gargamarruni*. The weekly market of the itinerant vendors is held near the sports' fields, every Friday.

All kinds of foodstuffs, clothes and household articles are sold there.

It is impossible to describe the tourist spots and monuments of Agrigento without taking into consideration the configuration of the terrain and the layout of the city, which impose a division between the medieval and modern quarters and the ancient city proper (Valley of the Temples).

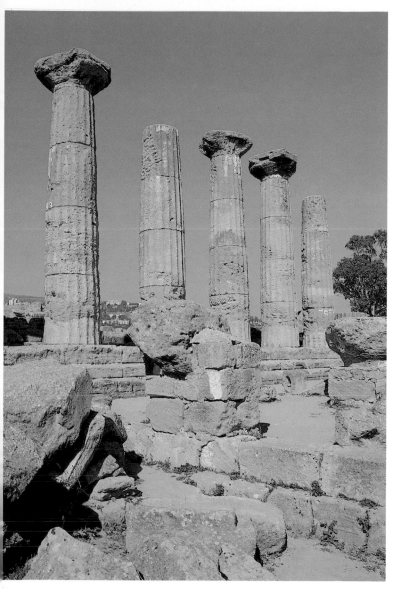

Some of the remaining columns from the Temple of Hercules.

THE VALLEY OF THE TEMPLES

The exciting architectural remains of the ancient city are scattered over this valley, which is unique for the vastness of its views and the richness of its landscape, setting and monuments. The whole creates an intense Mediterranean vista, made almost fairylike by the play of colours, the intense scent of flowers and earth and the luminous presence of the sea which allays, with its constant breezes, the fierce rays of the Sicilian sun. From December to March the flowering of the almonds gives the place the appearance of a enchanted dream, celebrated with fairs and popular festivities. The temple zone can be reached by car from the state highroad and on foot from the Piazza Marconi in the centre of town.

Hellenistic-Roman Quarter - This is a quite large section of an ancient town, settled in the fourth to third centuries B.C.; its most recent buildings date from the fourth to fifth centuries A.D. Roads running in the four main directions form a grid on which stand the ancient houses, shops and other buildings. Some decorative mosaic floors have been preserved,

61

The remains of the Temple of Olympian Zeus, fifth century B.C.

together with stretches of intonacoed wall with paintings on them. The type of decoration gives us an idea of the dates of the extensive ruins, which stretch from the Republican to the Imperial periods (first, second and third century A.D.). Over the whole vast area we can see the remains of sewerage and water pipes. In this ancient residential area, there are three blocks and a few separate houses we may wish to see in particular. These include the **House of the Aphrodites**, **House of the Diamond Mosaic**, **House of the Peristyle** (a typical example of a luxurious home with attached baths), **House of the Gazzelle** (which takes its name from the gazelle represented in the floor mosaics, now in the Museum), **House of the Abstract Master**, rich in admirable mosaics, and the **House of the Portico**.

Giacatello Hypogeum - This is reached by a small road starting from the Archaeological Museum and following the stream of the same name. It is very probably an ancient (fifth century B.C.) water reservoir; its appearance today is that of a vast underground room like a square cistern, with skylights and a lining of beaten earth.

Church of San Nicola - This building as we see it today goes back to the thirteenth century; it was built by the Cistercians on a site where there were the remains of ancient Greek and Roman buildings and where monastic communities had settled and built a first church dedicated to St. Nicholas. The church, between Romanesque and Gothic in style, has a fine portal in the façade; the *interior* has a single nave. It contains a Greek sarcophagus with carvings representing the *myth of Phaedra*, held to be a Roman work of the second to third centuries A.D. and once kept in the Aula Capitolare of the Cathedral. We should particularly note the apse, which is distinguished for its row of little blind arches of Romanesque type and powerful stone ogival vault.
Close by, near the remains of a theatre building dug out of the rock, is the **Oratory of Phalaris**, a temple building with a small hexedra rising on a podium.

Temple of Hercules - Among the ruins of this temple stand the eight columns raised again, in 1924, out of the 44 that adorned the building. It is a Doric temple, almost certainly the most ancient of the temples of Agrigento, and dates from the sixth century B.C. It is distinguished for the originality of its structure, of which three of the tall steps bounding the rectangular platform remain.
The *Herakleion* was originally a peripteral temple with six columns; its cornice, originally of clay, was later replaced by one in stone, decorated with lion heads and considerably restored during Roman times. In the westernmost zone of the excavations we find the **Tomb of Theron**, of

the Roman period (first century B.C.), near the ancient **Porta Aurea** (Golden Gate) in a beautiful landscape setting, and the remains of the ancient **Temple of Aesculapius** (fifth century B.C.), the style of which is pure Doric.

Temple of Olympian Zeus - Many visible vestiges remain of the ancient temple of Zeus (Jupiter), built in the fifth century B.C. to celebrate the victory of the Carthaginians at Himera. The building, attacked by repeated earthquakes and almost entirely razed by the Carthaginians at the end of the fifth century B.C., was despoiled right up to the end of the seventeenth century for materials to be used in buildings and public works. The *Olympeion* was a pseudo-peripteral temple which had, instead of a peristyle, a powerful wall with semi-columns at intervals where the giant figures of the *Telamons* stood. These figures had the function of helping to support the massive structure of the entablature; a copy of one of them, restored, can be seen on the ground in the temple, while the original has been transferred to the Archaeological Museum. In ancient times this temple was believed to be second in size only to the Cyclopean Temple of Diana at Ephesus.

Temple of Castor and Pollux - The four columns which for a long time have been the emblem of Agrigento stand as we see them today thanks to the restoration carried out in the last century by the sculptor V. Villareale and the architect S. Cavallari. They are all that is left of a temple built in the fifth century B.C., and are marked by the admirable decoration of the architraves, in Hellenistic-Roman style.
In this area have also been found the remains of religious buildings and

The Temple of Castor and Pollux, fifth century B.C., the emblem of the town.

Two views of the majestic Temple of Concordia, which is in an excellent state of preservation.

very ancient sanctuaries (going back as far as the sixth century B.C.) dedicated to Demeter and Persephone and known as a whole as the **Sanctuary of the Cthonic Divinities**.

In the western part of the Valley of the Temples are the ruins of the **Temple of Vulcan**, a Doric building dating from the fifth century B.C.

Temple of Concordia - To reach this temple we pass by the **Villa Aurea** (in the direction of the excavations), near which are the **Roman necropolis of Giambertoni** (second century B.C. to fourth century A.D.) the remains of a Byzantine necropolis and the catacombs called **Grotta di Fragapane** (fourth century A.D.).

A splendid example of Doric architecture, and one of the greatest attractions and archaeological treasures in Sicily, the temple has come down to us in an excellent state of conservation, although the wear of centuries has eroded the structure of the shell-limestone tufa of which it is built and stripped it of its stucco coating.

The building, which is similar in structure and colour to the Temple of Theseus at Athens, was originally dedicated to Castor and Pollux and built, in all probability, in the time of Theron (fifth century B.C.). It is a hexastyle peripteral temple with 34 columns standing on a platform with four steps up to it. It was converted into a Christian basilica in the sixth century; the arched openings in the walls of the cella are of that period.

Temple of Juno Lacinia - This also is a hexastyle peripteral temple in pure Doric mould; it is the best preserved of the temples of Agrigento after the Temple of Concordia. Built around the middle of the fifth century B.C., it was soon after damaged by a fire which led to its restoration in Roman times. Of the original building 25 columns are left, some of them truncated. Particularly imposing is the colonnade on the north side supporting the powerful architrave.

Rock Sanctuary of Demeter - This very ancient building, dug out of the rock around the seventh century B.C., dates from before the Greek civilization; it overlooks an area rich in **fortifications** erected by the Greeks, below which is the ancient **Gela Gate**, where objects connected with the cult of the Cthonic Divinities have been found. Uphill from the Sanctuary of Demeter is a fifth century **Doric temple** also dedicated to her; in medieval times it was converted into a church dedicated to San Biagio.

One of the Telamons of the Temple of Olympian Zeus in Agrigento.

Regional Archaeological Museum - Counted among the biggest and best arranged museum collections of this kind in Sicily, the Archaeological Museum of Agrigento exhibits important finds from the town and from other zones nearby.

In **Room I** we find information of topographical and cartographical interest on the ancient settlement of Agrigento and materials from classical times.

Room II displays finds from prehistoric times, especially the Aeneolithic period and the Bronze and Iron Ages, and materials from Gela, the necropolis of Montelusa and other necropolises in the region, dating from the seventh to sixth centuries B.C.

In **Room III** is a valuable collection of pottery from the fifth to third centuries B.C., among which the typical Attic vases and the Greek-Italiot vases stand out. Of particular interest is the crater with a representation of the myth of *Perseus and Andromeda* on it (fifth century B.C.).

In **Room IV** we can see interesting fragments of temples, stone water spouts with lion heads and other ornaments.

Room V brings together materials from the Agrigento temple complex, including sculptures from the Greek, Hellenistic and Siceliot periods.

In **Room VI**, which is dedicated to the Temple of Olympian Zeus, the most important item is the reconstruction, out of the original materials, of the gigantic *Telamon* (about eight metres) which once stood in the temple; it was one of a series and the heads from some of the others can also be seen in this room.

In **Room VII** we find interesting materials from the Hellenistic-Roman quarter, especially the *emblemata* from the mosaic floors that adorned some of the buildings.

Room VIII contains a collection of inscriptions, where we notice especially those from Agrigento monuments of the Greek age.

In **Room IX** (after obtaining permission to enter) we can see gold, silver and bronze coins from the classical to medieval periods. Most noteworthy are the silver Agrigentum coins of the fifth century B.C., with interesting figures on them.

Room X contains an admirable marble sculpture of an Ephebus, a Greek original of the fifth century B.C.

In **Room XI** are finds from the ancient necropolises in the Agrigento area.

Rooms XII-XIII display prehistoric finds and materials from the necropolises and excavation zones in the province and bordering regions. The most important are those from the Agrigento necropolis of Sant'Angelo Muxaro.

Room XIV contains material of topographical interest from some centres round Agrigento.

Room XV contains a variety of materials from Gela, among which we note particularly an original Greek crater from the fifth century B.C. with red figures representing the *Battle of the Amazons*.

Rooms XVI-XVII contain finds from the necropolises and the ancient Nissene settlements, with topographically interesting representations of the province of Caltanissetta.

Room XVIII (which can be visited by permission) houses the so-called *Museo di Seconda Scelta* (Second Choice Museum).

In **Room XIX** temporary exhibitions are held.

Luigi Pirandello

*The Sicilian writer and playwright Luigi Pirandello is considered one of the most important representatives of literary and theatrical culture at the turn of the century. Born at Girgenti in 1867, he went to school in Palermo where he subsequently enrolled in university courses in the faculties of Law and Letters. He moved to Rome, continued his studies in the humanities and published a collection of poems (*Mal Giocondo, 1889). Having graduated in Glottology in Germany, he returned to Rome, and wrote the poems in the collection* Amori senza Amore, *a prelude to his great story-writing activity which produced the* Novelle per un anno *(1922-1936).* L'Esclusa (1901) - *and even more his following works (* Il Fu Mattia Pascal, *1904;* Così è se vi pare, *1918;* Uno, nessuno, centomila, *1926) establish the qualities of Pirandello's prose, a curious mixture of realistic experiences and tormented intuitions about the meaninglessness of life. Between 1918 and 1927 Pirandello wrote plays such as* Il gioco delle parti, Ma non è una cosa seria *and above all the well known* Sei personaggi in cerca di autore (*"Six Characters in Search of an Author").* The founding of the* Teatro d'Arte *in Rome (1925) and the reception of the Nobel Prize for literature (1934) were milestones in the career of this great playwright, who died in Rome in 1936.*

The birthplace and tomb of the famous writer from Agrigento.

The sixteenth century Palazzo Steripinto.

SCIACCA

An important place for tourists and health seekers on the coast o
Agrigento, the little town of Sciacca spreads over hills sloping steeply t
the sea. Its Hellenistic origins go back to the time of the colonization o
Selinunte; the therapeutic properties of its thermal springs were recog
nized as early as the Roman period, when it was known as *Termae
Selinuntinae*, and later as *Aquae Larodes*. In the Middle Ages it belonged
first to the Arabs and then to the Normans, who reinforced its defense
works; it was disputed for a long time in the local wars which pitted vari
ous feudal potentates against each other. The **Aragonese walls**, of which
some stretches remain, go back to the sixteenth century.
The **Steripinto** is a fifteenth century building in Spanish plateresque
style, with original diamond-point ashlar-work, battlements and lance
windows.
Close by, near the **San Salvatore Gate** (sixteenth century), is the
Church of the Carmine, a building in Baroque style with a Gothic fron
ton on the façade.
On the opposite side of the street is the **Church of Santa Margherita**
originally built in the fourteenth century and remodelled in the sixteenth
century. The portal on the façade looks Gothic; the one on the side i
in Gothic-Renaissance style (fifteenth century) and is decorated with bas
reliefs by P. de Bonitate and F. Laurana. The stuccoes that adorn the in
terior are from the seventeenth century (O. Ferraro).
In the same street is the graceful **Casa Arone**, built in the fifteenth cen
tury, with elegant lancet windows in its façade.
The **Duomo** was first built in the Norman period (twelfth century), bu
was completely altered in the eighteenth century. What is left of the origi
nal construction is the apse. On the façade and inside the Cathedral ar

68

many sculptures, some of which are the work of Antonello and Domenico Gagini.

A Picture Gallery and a collection of coins have recently been arranged in the nearby **Casa Scaglione**.

On the way to the **Luna Castle**, a building of the second half of the fourteenth century of which only the walls and a cylindrical tower remain, is a small Romanesque (twelfth century) church called after **San Nicolò**, which has a façade with strong lines and three small apses at the back.

In the upper part of the town is the Piazza G. Noceto, where we find the sixteenth century **Church of San Michele** and the **San Calogero Gate**, opening on to what was the city perimeter in the sixteenth century.

On nearby **Mount San Calogero**, which looks down on the town from its height of 388 meters, are the **Stufe di San Calogero**, vents releasing radioactive steam that is utilized in therapy. The discovery of prehistoric material in the zone supports the hypothesis that the 'stufe' (ovens) were already in use in very ancient times.

At the top of the hill, in a very fine natural and panoramic situation, is the Sanctuary of San Calogero, which houses an admirable *Statue of St. Calogero* by G. Gagini (first half of the sixteenth century).

PALMA DI MONTECHIARO

This town lies on the lower slopes of Mount Pozzillo, near the coast. Ancient finds from a cave near the place demonstrate that human beings lived there already in prehistoric times. A distinguishing feature of the town is that it was built in the seventeenth century by Carlo Tomasi di Lampedusa, an ancestor of the author of the novel *Il Gattopardo*.

The **Chiesa Madre** has a certain interest; it has Baroque traits, as do some other buildings.

On the nearby **Marina** we can seen the **Castle of the Princes of Lampedusa**.

Near the town, high up on a rock overlooking the sea, rises the **Castle of Montechiaro** (fourteenth century).

Also in the surroundings are the seventeenth century **Fortress of San Carlo** and the fifteenth century **Castellazzo di Palma**.

The ancient convent of SS. Rosario.

69

Panoramic view of the island of Lampedusa.

ISLAND OF LAMPEDUSA

The largest of the Pelagian islands is also the nearest Italian island to the coast of North Africa, and is 133 meters high at its highest point. The first human settlements there date from prehistoric times, which is demonstrated by findings from the Bronze Age and some megalithic constructions. Already known to the Romans (as *Lopadusa*) it was the scene of a naval battle between Arabs and Byzantines. For a long time it had no permanent inhabitants, but was settled again in the time of Ferdinand II. During the Second World War it was a centre for Allied military manoeuvres. In very recent times it was touched by Libyan missiles during an acute international crisis.

Lampedusa lies on a harbour and is the only town worth mentioning; the sea coasts of the island are sheer cliffs and it is covered in typical Mediterranean scrub. The inhabitants are mostly employed in fishing, especially for sponges. Agriculture is made very difficult by lack of water.

ISLAND OF LINOSA

This is the first island we come to in the Straits of Sicily, and constitutes, together with Lampedusa and the desert rock Lampione, the Pelagian archipelago proper. Known in ancient times as *Aetusa* (Algusa), it is obviously of volcanic origin. Its highest hill, Mount Vulcano, measures 195 meters. The only town of any size is **Linosa**, a typical agricultural and fishing settlement.

Aerial view of the island of Linosa.

CALTANISSETTA

Historical Note - The city lies in the upper part of the Valle del Salso, on the southern slopes of Mount San Giuliano, which is the geometrical centre of Sicily. Its origins are remote, and seem to date from a period earlier than the Classical age, when a *Nissa* is heard of. The Saracens added the prefix *Kalat*, and the placename acquired the strange meaning of "castle of women". Having come under the Normans in the second half of the eleventh century, it was later Aragonese and then a feud of the Lancias, the Aragonese Dukes of Randazzo and the Moncadas, who held it for four centuries.

The present Caltanissetta, as well as being the administrative centre of a province, has deeply rooted craft traditions and is taking its place as a tourist resort on the strength of the rediscovery and promotion of some folk festivities. One of these is the Holy Thursday Procession, when the Misteri, large papier-mâché figures representing the Passion of Christ, are carried through the streets.

The town is surrounded by a fertile agricultural district and is the centre of Sicilian mining territory. The mines were very active in the thirties, but although they still produce a considerable quantity of sulphur and of potassium and manganese salts, they have declined now that new sources of energy have been found.

The places where the people of Caltanissetta prefer to go for their evening walks are along Corso Umberto, in the most ancient part of the town, and along the Viale della Regione in the more recently built part. The most typical items of local craftsmanship include the wood carvings, the pottery and the traditional angalarruni (Jew's harps). One of the most characteristic markets is the Pescheria, which offers fish, vegetables, fruit and typical Sicilian cheeses.

Duomo - The Cathedral was begun in the second half of the sixteenth century and finished in the first half of the following century. The *façade*, which is quite wide, is in two tiers, adorned by pilasters and framed between two bell towers, and goes back to the first half of the last century.

The **interior**, sumptuous and solemn, has marked eighteenth century rococo traits. There are many stuccoes which provide a florid frame for the numerous frescoes by the Flemish artist Guglielmo Borremans. Powerful pillars supporting the arched vaults divide the interior space of the church into a nave and two aisles. Works of art it contains include

Internal view of the Baroque style Cathedral.

an altar-piece by Borremans over the high altar, representing the *Immaculate Virgin with Saints*, a seventeenth century painting in the first chapel on the right representing the *Baptism of Jesus*, and a wooden statue of the Archangel Michael, a seventeenth century work by Stefano Li Volsi in a chapel to the right of high altar. An admirable *Virgin of the Carmen* by Filippo Paladino hangs above the altar in the left transept.

Opposite the Duomo, on the other side of Piazza Garibaldi (where we see the modern *Fountain of Neptune* with bronze sculptures by Tripisciano), is the tall, late nineteenth century façade of the Church of San Sebastiano, divided vertically into three tiers.

Piazza Garibaldi with the Church of San Sebastiano.

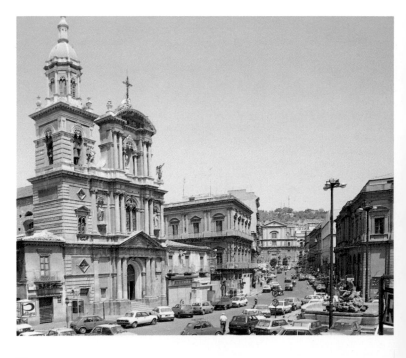

GELA

An important industrial and commercial town, Gela stands at the mouth of the river of the same name, on the southern coast of Sicily. The town is developing as a bathing resort for tourists, and is also known because of the ANIC petrochemical complex there. Already settled in prehistoric times, it is a city of Doric origin, founded by settlers from Rhodes and Crete (seventh century B.C.). Devastated in the fifth century B.C. by the Carthaginian militia, it was rebuilt a century later by Timoleon. In the third century B.C. the city was razed by the Mamertines and fell into oblivion until the first half of the thirteenth century when, under Frederick II, it rose again as *Terranova*. It got its old name back only in 1928. On Good Friday a picturesque *Crucifixion* pageant is held there.

In the eastern part of the town, on the site of the ancient acropolis, the remains of the **Timoleon Quarter** have been brought to light. They date from the fourth century B.C.; below them are traces of even more ancient constructions. In the **Parco della Rimembranza** below, we can see the base and the ruins of a *Doric temple* of the fifth century B.C. and the more ancient *Temple of Athena* (sixth century B.C.). This was probably a peripteral structure, but little is left of it besides the base; the fine clay ornaments found on the site were taken to the Syracuse Museum. From the nearby look-out point we can admire a wide panorama of the plain of Gela.

Also in the same area is the **Archaeological Museum**, the various sections of which display valuable archaeological finds from this district and surrounding districts. In the first section, where we find material from the prehistoric and archaic periods, the most interesting item is the fifth century *terracotta horse head*. In the second section are finds from sanctuaries in the area and from the acropolis; a clay statuette of *Demeter* and statuettes of *Athena seated* stand out among the rest. The third section contains finds from ancient settlements outside the town, sanctuaries outside the acropolis and ancient ceramic objects and fragments (seventh to fourth centuries B.C.). In the fourth section are materials connected with the city, from the fourth to third centuries B.C., finds from Cape Soprano, inscriptions and ancient ceramic graffiti (sixth to fifth centuries B.C.). The fifth section displays items from sanctuaries outside the walls and ancient earthenware vases dating from the fifth century B.C. In the same section are funerary objects from the ancient Greek necropolises. The seventh

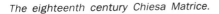

The eighteenth century Chiesa Matrice.

The remains of the archaeological area of Gela, fourth century B.C..

section consists of materials from Gela and its surroundings. The eighth section provides a glimpse of the city in the Early Christian and Medieval ages. In the ninth section are private collections, terracottas and vases of Attic origin. The museum also contains a fine *numismatic collection* with Siceliot and Athenian coins.

Further important vestiges of the ancient city can be seen at **Cape Soprano**, where quite well preserved remains of **fortifications** dating from the fifth and fourth centuries B.C. are scattered. These fortificatons were restored at the time when Timoleon rebuilt the town in the fourth century B.C., and consist of blocks of stone below with unbaked bricks above. From the way the ruins lie it is possible to deduce the original layout of the complex, which included a number of towers alternating with sentry beats.

Not far away are the remains of the **Greek baths** (fourth century B.C.) where we can see clearly the arrangement of the bathing pools and the system used to heat the water.

The **Chiesa Matrice** on Piazza Umberto I in the centre of town is worth seeing; it is an eighteenth century building with a façade in Neo-Classical style.

To the north of Gela is the **Lago del Disueri**, an artificial basin built to irrigate the plain below. On the outcrops above it "oven" type Sicilian tombs have been found that once belonged to an extensive prehistoric necropolis.

Ancient ruins, dating from the fourth century B.C. and belonging to a settlement of indigenous people, have come to light on nearby **Mount Bubonia**.

ENNA

Historical Note - The city competes with nearby Caltanissetta to be considered the geometrical centre of Sicily. Because of its central position on the island it was called even in ancient times the *Navel of Sicily*. Of very ancient origin, *Henna* was a Sicanian centre where a cult similar to that of Demeter developed. At the time of the Greek colonization, the city succeeded in retaining a certain autonomy, which was challenged first by Agathocles of Syracuse (fourth century B.C.) and then by Carthage. It became a Roman possession and paid back with severe repression the slave revolt that occurred in the second century B.C. A *municipium* during the Imperial age, it was conquered by the Byzantines on the decline of Roman power. Because of its strategic position, which made it practically impregnable, it resisted the Arabs for a long time, and was occupied by them only after a siege lasting more than twenty years, in 859. Named by its new rulers *Kasrlanna*, the city went through a period of prosperity which lasted until the advent of the Normans (eleventh century). In following centuries, now called *Castrum Iohannis*, it became a

A nocturnal panorama at Enna.

75

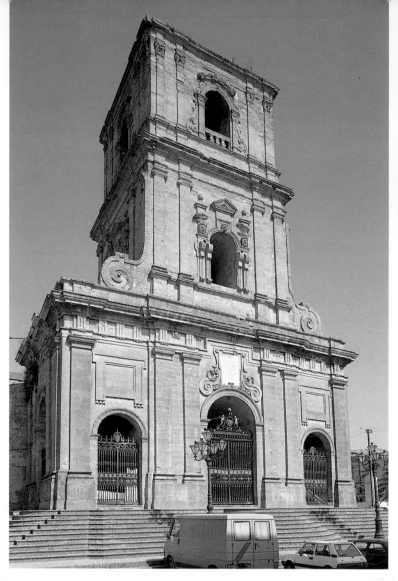

The façade of the fourteenth century Cathedral.

possession of Angevins and Aragonese, according to the vicissitudes of Sicilian history. Until 1926 the city kept the name of Castrogiovanni, and then returned to its original name and was made capital of its province. The Enna of our time rises at the top of a terraced mountain spur, a highly panoramic setting in the middle of an agricultural district where mining activities also prosper. Over the last ten years its tourist trade has become substantial; the *"balcony of Sicily"* is an important base for sightseeing in the interesting centres of the province. The town, which has the distinction of being the highest provincial capital in Italy (931 meters), attracts the visitor's attention by its human scale, which makes it easy to discover the beauties of its architecture and the great interest of its layout and its streets.

Some of the places where people meet are Via Roma, Piazza Vittorio Emanuele and Piazza Umberto I. Every day in Via Mercato San Antonio a food market is held where the typical local sausages and cheeses can be bought. The market for fruit and vegetables and some kinds of clothing is held weekly in Piazza Europa. Outstanding among typical craft products are articles in wrought iron, copper and other alloys, lace, embroidery and the ubiquitous pottery. Speaking of folk festivities, the Easter Week Processions are very important; the hooded members of the various Confraternities and Societies take part in them.

Duomo - The Cathedral dates from the fourteenth century, having been built in the middle of the Aragonese period. Seriously damaged by fire in the second half of the fifteenth century, it was rebuilt in the Baroque age (seventeenth century). The powerful *façade* looks on to a sweeping flight of steps and has a porch with a seventeenth century tower above it. The apse is in three parts and in Gothic style. A sixteenth century portal by Gagini on the right side is worth noting; it contains a marble bas-relief representing St. Martin and the Beggar, brought there from an old church in the Castello di Lombardia.

The dramatic *interior* has a nave and two aisles divided by powerful pillars supporting ogival arches. In the left aisle we observe the sixteenth century *holy-water stoup*, the *pulpit* carved by G. Gallina (seventeenth century), and the admirable baptismal font. The coffered wooden ceiling is also worth noting. In the presbytery we find paintings by F. Paladino (seventeenth century). In the left apse is the ***Chapel of the Sacrament***, while in the right is the ***Chapel of the Virgin of the Visitation***, originally of the eighteenth century. Finally, there are many paintings by the Flemish artist G. Borremans (eighteenth century).

Church of San Francesco - Originally built in the fifteenth century, this church has been several times altered and incorporates in the apse a tower once belonging to the Palazzo dei Chiaramonte. A flight of steps leads to the portico on the side of the building; the *interior* preserves a finely made eighteenth century wooden choir, a fifteenth century wooden Crucifix and an Adoration of the Magi attributed to the Flemish artist S. de Wobreck.

Church of the Carmine - This seventeenth century church has a tower believed to be of very ancient origin (tenth century). In the *interior* we find interesting works of art, among them a Crucifixion painted on canvas and various other paintings; worth mentioning is an Ecstasy of St. Teresa of Avila attributed to Saverio Marchese.

Church of San Tommaso - The important features of this church include the fifteenth century *portico*, in Catalan-Gothic style, and the *tower* (tenth century), which was once part of the complex system of defense towers of Enna. The *interior* of the building has clean lines. On the high altar is an admirable sixteenth century marble icon attributed to the artist G. Mancino from Carrara, which represents the Madonna and Child in a niche surrounded by Saints.

Torre di San Giovanni - This was the most ancient church in the city. Its bell tower has typically fifteenth century features, with Gothic traits in the cut and ornamentation of the windows and Arab traits in the small dome that crowns the building. Close by is the ***Church of San Benedetto***, of the Baroque period.

The imposing "Castello di Lombardia".

A partial view of the "Castello di Lombardia" and the tower of Frederick II.

Church of Santa Chiara - This monumental seventeenth century church in Baroque style looks down on an imposing flight of steps. At first intended as a church for the Jesuits, it is a grandiose building and possesses a fine painting attributed to the sixteenth-seventeenth century artist known as Zoppo di Gangi, representing the Madonna delle Grazie. We should notice the nineteenth century ceramic floor and some majolica works. In the eighteenth century the church passed to the order of the Poor Clares.

Castello di Lombardia - This ancient building in the highest part of the town was probably built earlier than the Swabian period, when it is usually held to have originated. A defense bastion of quite complex structure, it is one of the best examples of Castilian architecture in Sicily. Its name was given to it in Norman times, and refers to a garrison of Lombard cavalry. Only six towers remain of the twenty that once existed; one of the most important is the ***Pisan Tower***, which is crowned by a battlemented structure. In one of the courtyards an open-air theatre has been built, and important performances are held there during the summer season. The ***Statue of Eunus*** outside the castle commemorates the slave revolt that occurred in Roman times.

Rocca di Cerere - This building rises in a high place not far from the Castello di Lombardia, and is an extremely ancient fort connected, since the remote past, with the cult of Ceres. This was very probably the site of a temple dedicated to the goddess of which the town possesses archaeological vestiges. From the top of the fort we can enjoy a wide panoramic view of the surroundings and the valley through which the Dittaino river runs.

Torre di Federico - This strange, octagonal structure rises in the middle of the public gardens and dates from the thirteenth century, when it was probably part of a larger and more important castle. The lines of the solid building are typical of Castilian architecture of the time of Frederick and can also be seen in other regions; it must have been part of the complex fortifications of Castrogiovianni, most likely connected with the Castello di Lombardia itself.

Palazzo Pollicarini - This town house has the characteristics of a medieval fortitied palace, with elements of 15th century Castilian-Gothic style.

PIAZZA ARMERINA

Although it is situated inland, Piazza Armerina is one of Sicily's most important tourist resorts. It lies along a ridge in the Erei mountains, in a setting of great natural beauty and near an area which has great archaeological interest because one of the finest Roman villas that have come down to us still stands there. Once known as *Platia*, it developed as a marketplace where the Lombard militia spent their money, which would explain its strange name. According to some sources it already existed before the Roman colonization, when it was known as *Hibla*. In the Middle Ages it suffered various vicissitudes, including being destroyed in the second half of the twelfth century by William the Bad. Later, Piazza Armerina competed for a long time with Enna to become the Bishop's See, succeeding in this only in the first half of the nineteenth century. The *Palio dei Normanni*, which is held in August, is the most important of the folk festivities of the town.

The powerful outline of the ***Duomo*** is the first sight we have of the town on approaching. A building with Baroque characteristics, it goes back to the seventeenth century and was built over a previous fifteenth century church. The façade overlooks a flight of steps and has sixteenth century Mannerist features and a strange portal adorned with spiral tufa columns in Renaissance taste. The attached bell tower has Catalan-Gothic traits and belonged to the old fifteenth century building. The magnificent Baroque interior is crowned by a spectacular dome; on the high altar is a precious silver tabernacle with a splendid Byzantine painting of the *Holy Virgin of Victory*, while on the side walls are sixteenth century paintings by Zoppo di Gangi. An admirable arch attributed to A. Gagini to the right of the entrance contains the *baptismal font*. In the chapel on the left is a fine wooden *Crucifix* attributed to the Maestro della Croce di Piazza Armerina (fifteenth century), together with a fifteenth century *Madonna and Child*, of Umbrian origin. Paintings in the church include works by F. Paladino, G. Martorana and J. Ligozzi. In the attached ***Cathedral***

A panoramic view of the town.

Museum we can see fine bas-reliefs, precious reliquaries, silver objects and ancient Christmas cribs.

The **Church of the Gran Priorato di Sant'Andrea** is from the twelfth century and is counted among the most ancient churches in the town. It has the distinctive features of medieval architecture, including a portal with Arab and Norman stylistic motifs.

Among other churches worth noting, we find the seventeenth century **Church of Fundrò**, which has a fine tufa portal with Baroque decorations, the ancient Gothic **Church of the Commenda** (twelfth century), once seat of the *Order of the Knights of Jerusalem and Malta*, the seventeenth century **Church of Santo Stefano** and the **Church of San Pietro** (seventeenth century), which has sculptures from the workshop of the Gagini and an eighteenth century wooden ceiling.

The **Aragonese Castle** was built during the fourteenth century under Martin I of Aragon; it is a structure with a square base and corner towers, which stands out among the buildings of the town.

We must mention, finally, the **Palazzo Trigona** (eighteenth century), which has both Renaissance and Baroque features, and the so-called **Palazzo di Città** (City Palace), an eighteenth century edifice built as a Benedictine monastery, in which we can admire frescoes by G. Martorana.

The **Roman Villa of Casale** remains, however, the most important sight to see in the region, and is one of the finest examples of Roman country dwellings on the island. It was built in the third-fourth century B.C., and its happiest time was between the fourth and fifth centuries A.D., just before the devastations wrought by the barbarians. The splendour of the mosaic decorations in the floors has made this ancient Roman villa famous all over the world. It was brought to light in the late twenties, and the work of excavating it is not yet complete. The wide use of mosaics to beautify the floors and walls of the extraordinary complex gives us an important insight into mosaic technique; the work was very probably

The Roman villa at Casale and a detail of the mosaic of the gymnasium inside.

Some details of the mosaics of the "Little Circus", the "Fishing Room" and the "Corridor of the Great Hunt".

done by artists of North African origin, and is one of the finest examples existing of this type of decoration, widely used by the Romans wherever they went.

The entrance leads to an **Atrium** of poligonal plan with a colonnade, a fountain in the centre and stretches of mosaic paving. We continue through the **Vestibule**, which has a fine mosaic in its floor, and come to the **Big Peristyle**, with a marble colonnade, a pool in the centre and numerous mosaic decorations, which are a feature also of the rooms on the north side. Among these last the scene of the *Little hunt* is famous. The long **Ambulacrum of the great hunt** is rich in mosaic scenes celebrating the hunting and capture of wild animals. On the lower side of the Big Peristyle is the room with the well known scene of *Women gymnasts*. Known also as the **Room of the Ten Girls**, it attracts our attention with its figures of young girls, dressed in scanty costumes (comparable to the modern bikini), playing gymnastic games.

In an adjacent room with a fountain in the middle is a scene with *Orpheus*. On the east side of the Ambulacrum of the great hunt is a room similar to a basilica with an apse where company must have been received. To the south of this was the part of the house used for living in, also rich in fine mosaic decorations. Scenes with mythological subjects adorn also the rooms on the east side of the upper part of the already mentioned Ambulacrum. Coming to the **Elliptical Peristyle**, a courtyard with a portico and fountain in the centre, we can see the mosaics in the rooms that open on to it, which represent "Amorini" intent on fishing and picking grapes. We then come to the **Triclinium**, an interesting room with three apses and mosaics with mythological scenes. Returning to the Atrium, we come to the **Salone del Circo** (Hall of the Circus), so called for its mosaics, which represent scenes of competitions in the Circus Maximus in Rome. We then go on to the baths, where we can distinguish the different rooms, the **Frigidarium**, the **Tepidarium** and the **Calidarium**, and their respective heating systems.

MORGANTINA

The big village of Aidone is situated in a beautiful natural setting, with a fine view, on the slopes of the Erei mountains, not far from Piazza Armerina. It developed during the Arab period, in a previously settled area, and is known through the history of its castle, which from the Norman age on came under the control of various feudal lords.

The Church of Santa Maria la Cava has a bell tower which was once used for defense purposes. Of the fourteenth century building (it was built in the Aragonese period) only the apse remains.

Among other buildings worth noting we should mention the sixteenth century Church of San Michele and the Church of Sant'Anna which contains an admirably crafted Crucifix attributed to Fra Umile da Petralia. Of great interest is the **Antiquarium** which has been set up in a building which was once a Capucine monastery. Materials found in nearby **Morgantina** are exhibited there. Morgantina is a very important archaeological zone, discovered in the fifties in the locality of Serra d'Orlando. Probably founded by Chalcidian colonists from Catania in the sixth century B.C., it was important in the Hellenistic and Roman periods, but went into a rapid and definitive decline in the first century B.C.

What has been brought to light of the ancient settlement is the **Agora** which was built on two levels and included the **Macellum**, a Roman shopping centre, the **Bouleuterion**, the **Gymnasium**, the **Theatre**, the remains of rich houses with mosaic decorations, vestiges of a **Sanctuary** dedicated to the cult of the gods of the underworld, and a building used as a granary. The whole surrounding zone is scattered with ruins and partially buried remains, such as those of the **Sanctuary of Demeter and Kore**. On a nearby hill, traces of the ancient acropolis and a settlement devastated in the fifth century B.C. have been found.

The remains of the ancient town, founded in the sixth century B.C.

RAGUSA

Historical Note - This town rises on the southern spurs of the Hyblaean (Ibla) Hills, in a region marked by the complexity of its system of river valleys, which constrict the towns of *Ragusa* and *Ibla* between the depressions dug out by the San Leonardo and San Domenico streams, tributaries of the Irminio catchment basin. Archaeological studies and the existence of ancient tombs dug into the rock support the theory that the place has been inhabited since prehistoric times, to be exact since the Bronze Age. This was certainly the site of the Sicel town known as *Hybla Heraea*, which established relations with Greek settlers from Camarina, a centre founded by Syracuse. We have little information about the Roman *Hibla*, which was probably razed by the Vandals.

Rebuilt by Dalmatian colonists from Ragusa, who gave it the name of their native place (seventh century A.D.), it was fortified in the Byzantine age by a ring wall, in order to resist the frequent raids of Saracen pirates. In the first half of the ninth century Ragusa fell into Arab hands. With the coming of the Normans, in the eleventh century, it was made a county, and a century later its jurisdiction was extended to include Modica. It became a feud of the Chiaramontes, then passed into the hands of the Aragonese and the Henriquez. Seriously damaged by the earthquake of 1542 and almost destroyed by that of 1693, its buildings and layout were substantially transformed. During the wars of the Risorgimento the town made an important contribution to the struggle against the Bourbons. In 1865 an administrative unit with the name of *Ragusa Ibla* was formed, comprising the oldest part of the town, while the new part, called *Ragusa Superiore*, developed more and more. In 1926 the two parts were definitively reunited, and the following year, on this basis, a new province was born.

The Ragusa of our own days consists of two quite separate urban centres. On the eastern spur rises *Ibla*, the layout and buildings of which obviously spring from a medieval matrix. To the west spreads *Ragusa*, which is modern in appearance and has wide streets laid out in a regular grid pattern. The city has an active industrial sector and is connected in particular with the oil industry, especially with processing petrochemicals, and with the plastic, metallurgical and food industries. Craft activities are highly developed, producing ceramics decorated with scenes of Sicilian life, wrought iron objects, hand-worked embroideries and silks, yarns and straw- and wicker-work.

Panorama of the town.

One of the most typical folk festivals that should be mentioned is the Processione dei Misteri, which is held during the Good Friday celebrations; devotees carry in the procession the "Misteri", carved figures representing the characters in Christ's Passion.

The central Via Roma is the citizens' traditional meeting place; in an adjacent road and in Piazza San Giovanni the most important shops are situated. The weekly market is held on Thursdays in Piazza Solferino. Goods on sale range from clothing to linen and household articles. Fruit and vegetables can be bought there, and specialities such as the tasty local "caciocavallo" (a strong cheese), with or without pepper, and thyme honey from the Ibla region.

Cathedral - This is a vigorous eighteenth century construction, named after St. John the Baptist; it stands on Piazza San Giovanni Battista, which is surrounded by a marble balustrade, in the newer part of the town. The elegant ***façade*** is patterned across its width on two tiers; in the lower tier it is divided up by powerful columns with ornate capitals. To the sides of the main portal are small twin fluted columns, which support an architectural arrangement of Baroque character, loaded with sculptures. To one side of the façade rises the tall and graceful bell tower, which is topped by a spire. Over the crossing of the nave rises a cupola supported by a poligonal tambour.

The ***interior*** is of the basilica type, with an aisled nave; the aisles open on to a series of chapels from the last century, adorned with artistic stuccoes. Behind the Cathedral stands the ***Casa Canonica***, interesting for the architectural elegance of its eighteenth century lines.

Church of Santa Maria delle Scale - This church in the easternmost part of Ragusa takes its name from the charming flight of steps leading up to the ***Church of Santa Maria dell'Itria*** (eighteenth century). Santa Maria delle Scale was originally erected in the fifteenth to sixteenth centuries and largely rebuilt after the earthquake of 1693, preserving some parts of the original building, including the bell tower, the portal and the remains of the pulpit. The ***interior***, which has an aisled nave with Gothic and Renaissance characteristics, contains, on the second altar from the right in a chapel remodelled in the sixteenth century, a clay bas-relief of the first half of the same century representing the *Death of the Virgin*; it has the marks of the Gagini workshop.

Church of San Giorgio - A masterpiece of eighteenth century Baroque, this church with its Neo-Classical dome dominates the Ibla quarter. The design for this building was drawn up by R. Gagliardi, and it was completed in 1775. The dramatic *façade* looks down on a flight of steps and is designed on three orders, with columns marking the divisions and sculptural and flower motifs as adornments. Counted among the finest religious buildings in this part of Sicily, its *interior* has a nave divided from the two aisles by pilasters. In the *Sacristy* we can admire the valuable *Treasury* and some carvings from the workshop of the Gaginis.

Church of San Giuseppe - This Ibla church is also distinguished for the ornateness of its Baroque *façade*, which recalls motifs already present in the church of San Giorgio. This one also is the work of the architect Gagliardi. The *interior*, which has an unusual elliptical plan, also shows typical eighteenth century traits. Among the art works we should note the figure of St. Joseph, a refined sixteenth century carving.

Church of San Giorgio Vecchio - This church stands near the entrance to the park of the Giardino Ibleo. The admirable portal is of Catalan Gothic workmanship and dates from the second half of the fifteenth century, being the most conspicuous remnant of what was once the most important church in Ibla.

Church of the Cappuccini Vecchi - This church stands inside the Giardino Ibleo and preserves three admirable canvases attributed to Pietro Novelli and a panel of the sixteenth century. In the same public garden is the *Church of San Domenico*.

Church of the Immacolata - This church was built in the thirteenth century, together with the Monastery of the Frati Minori, and was later several times remodelled. Known at one time as San Francesco, the church has a fine bell tower and a portal of the Swabian period.

The Cathedral with its Baroque portal.

Palazzo Donnafugata - One of the most noteworthy examples of eighteenth-nineteenth century architecture, this palace contains the *Private collection of Barone Arezzo*. There are paintings attributed to Spagnoletto and Caravaggio; outstanding among the paintings is a *Madonna and Child* which many believe to be the work of Antonello da Messina, others of Antonio Solario. There are canvases also by Flemish artists, and valuable furnishings, vases and ceramics, some of which are of Eastern origin.

Palazzo Cosentini - A typical example of Baroque architecture, the distinctive feature of this palace is the shape of the balcony corbels.

Palazzo Battaglia - The distinguishing feature of this building is the considerable stylistic difference between its various sides.

Bridge of the Cappuccini - The tall, two-tiered spans of this bridge (first half of the nineteenth century) are a distinctive feature of the panorama of the new town, and contrast visibly with the modern lines of more recent constructions around the Cava di San Domenico.

Ibla Archaeological Museum - Set up during the sixties in rooms under the Hotel Mediterraneo, this museum displays archaeological finds from the province, ordered chronologically and by place.
Section I contains materials pertaining to prehistoric archaeology, from the Paleolithic to the Bronze Age; from this later time are the evidences of the *facies del Castelluccio*.
Section II shows us the findings from the Greek settlement of Camarina, which include many tomb furnishings from the ancient necropolises, clay objects from a fifth-third century B.C. kiln, and Greek and Roman ceramics.
In *Section III* we find the materials from Sicel sites of the Archaic and Classical periods, with particular reference to Monte Casasia, and findings from the necropolises of Rito and Castiglione.
Section IV concentrates on items which have come to light in the Hellenistic sites; we should note the finds from Scornavacche and the faithful reconstruction of a pottery workshop, using the original materials.
In *Section V* materials from the Roman period onward are arranged; of particular interest are the mosaics from an Early Christian place of worship found at Santa Croce Camarina, the finds from Caucana and the inscriptions from Comiso.
Section VI contains finds from various sites.

Surrounding area - The asphalt and petroleum mines just outside the city are interesting; the workings are open-cast or in galleries. Nearby is the petrochemical plant of ANIC. A Latomia with traces of an ancient Christian burial ground dating from the IVth-Vth century can be seen not far away.

MODICA

The large town of Modica lies at a short distance from the capital and can be divided into two different levels, *Modica Bassa* and *Modica Alta*. A city founded in ancient times, its origins are probably Greek and Sicel; in Roman times it was the prosperous *Motyka*, which was then called *Mohac* by the Arabs, who won possession of it in the ninth century. Important under the Normans, it later became a feud of the Chiaramontes, the Cabreras and the Henriquez. During the Risorgimento it was a hotbed of anti-Bourbon revolt.
The spectacular **Church of San Giorgio** (Cathedral) was originally constructed in the first half of the seventeenth century, but was entirely rebuilt in the eighteenth century. The magnificent three-tiered façade overlooks an imposing flight of steps; with its splendid Sicilian Baroque shapes, the exterior closely resembles the church of the same name in Ragusa. It was completed, in the upper tier, in the first half of the last century. The interior, a Latin cross in plan, is divided into a nave and

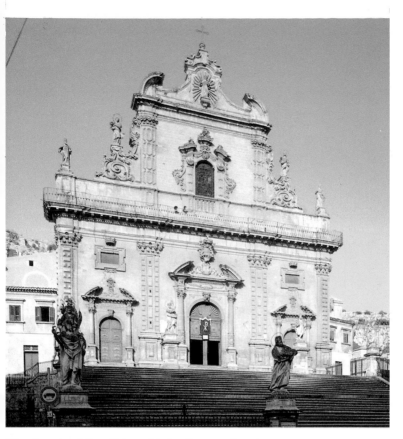

The Church of San Pietro with its Baroque façade.

as many as four aisles. In the apse is preserved a splendid sixteenth century polyptych very probably of the school of Antonello da Messina. We should notice the admirable stuccoes in the choir and the fine seventeenth century Baroque intaglios. The high altar, erected at the turn of the seventeenth and eighteenth centuries, is noteworthy for its refined silver engravings. Near one side entrance is a fine seventeenth century Assumption of the Madonna by Filippo Paladino. In the marble floor is a curious solar clock with the signs of the zodiac.

The **Church of San Pietro** originated in the fourteenth century but has eighteenth century characteristics, the result of reconstruction after two earthquakes during the seventeenth century. The exquisite two-tiered Baroque façade stands at the top of a spectacular flight of steps which is bordered by an iron fence and a number of admirable statues. The aisles, inside, are divided from the nave by majestic columns with splendid capitals of Corinthin type. We notice the statue of St. Peter and the Cripple by the Palermo artist P. Civiletti (end of the nineteenth century), and the Madonna of Trapani (right aisle, fourth altar), an admirable marble copy of the better known work by Laurana.

The **Church of Santa Maria di Betlem** goes back to the Norman period, but two portals are all that remain from that time. The rest is the result of remodelling and rebuilding. The interior has an aisled nave with a coffered ceiling from the second half of the last century; the marble floor is of the same date. Over the high altar is an eighteenth century Assumption of the Virgin by a local artist.

In the **Palazzo dei Mercedari** is the **Ibla Museum of Popular Arts and Traditions**, an interesting ethnographical glimpse of the crafts and peasant traditions of the place. In the adjacent **City Museum** we can see archaeological finds, fossils, examples of Greek and Early Christian art, and eighteenth and nineteenth century paintings. The **Palazzo De Leva** is marked by its fifteenth century Late Gothic portal.

The archaeological area of the town.

CAMARINA

The ruins of Camarina lie near the coast and are those of the city founded by the Syracusans in the sixth century B.C. and razed by the Romans in the third century B.C.

The most important vestiges include the **ring walls**, from the period of Timoleon, and the remains of the **Athenaion** (fifth century B.C.), the majestic temple of Athena which must at one time have been extremely impressive. The ruins of houses worth noticing include the **House of the Altar**, the **House of the Inscription** and the **House of the Merchant**. In an Antiquarium we find exhibited finds from the excavations, especially ceramics of Hellenistic type, ancient amphoras and material from the Necropolis of Rifriscolaro.

VITTORIA

A large rural and industrial centre, this town rises on a hill slope overlooking the valley of the Ippari. It is of seventeenth century origin, having been founded by the Colonna and Henriquez families, and its layout and buildings are in eighteenth century style.

The **Church of San Giovanni Battista** dates from the early eighteenth century. The powerful three-tiered façade is designed vertically; the interior is of the basilica type with an aisled nave with stucco, marble and gilt adornments. We should notice the wooden statue of the Baptist, some sculptures from the workshop of Serpotta and canvases by followers of P. Novelli.

The **Teatro Comunale** (City Theatre) stands out for the sumptuous character of its two-tiered Neo-Classical façade, with ornamental columns and admirable sculptures.

The **Church of Santa Maria delle Grazie** is the product of reconstruction in the second half of the eighteenth century. It has an elegant three-tiered façade with a clock in the middle, an eighteenth century high altar and some sculptures.

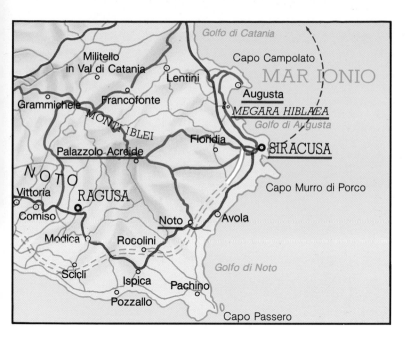

SYRACUSE

Historical Note - This city lies on the eastern coast of Sicily, in a charming setting with a picturesque harbour bounded by the Maddalena Peninsula and the island of Ortygia, which is practically connected to the mainland.

Syracuse was one of the most important colonies of Magna Grecia and according to reliable sources was founded by Corinthian settlers in 734 B.C. The first settlements were on the island of Ortygia, which became the original core of a much vaster inhabited area. In Classical times Syracuse was in fact made up of five towns: *Ortygia, Achradina, Tyche, Epipolae* and *Neapolis*. The city grew rapidly in prosperity and military strength, and soon became a magnetic centre of power for the entire Mediterranean basin, defeating the Carthaginians at Hymera (480 B.C.) with the help of Agrigentum. In 474 B.C. the Syracusans, under the command of Hiero, got the better of the Etruscans in the naval battle of Cumae, which placed a limit on the territorial expansion of the latter people toward the south. In 413 B.C. it was the turn of the Athenians to pay the price of opposing the might of Syracuse. Defeated and deported to the Latomie, the great majority of the prisoners met a terrible end. At the time of Dionysius the defenses of the city were fortified; Syracuse was on constant guard against attack by its eternal rival, Carthage. After various vicissitudes, the city was taken by subterfuge during the Second Punic Wars by the Romans (212 B.C.), who thus broke down the strenuous defense of the Syracusans. The latter had used, during the siege, the famous burning glasses invented by Archimedes, who met his death during the looting and violence that followed the Roman victory.

When the power of Rome declined, Syracuse suffered repeated attacks by Franks, Vandals and Goths; united with the Byzantine Empire (first half of the sixth century) it housed the court of Constans II, who was assassinated there in 668. Occupied by the Arabs in 878, it lost the important administrative role it had played up to then. In the second half of the eleventh century it was taken over by the Normans, who were followed by the Angevins and, after the events of the Sicilian Vespers, the Aragonese, who brought back to the town its prestige and authority. At the time of Charles V (sixteenth century), the city's defenses were further reinforced. Under the terms of the Treaty of Utrecht, Syracuse was hand-

The fifth century B.C. Greek theatre.

ed over to the Kingdom of Savoy, and then to the Austrians and Bourbons. In the first half of the nineteenth century, the city was the scene of a popular revolt, harshly put down by the Bourbon government, the consequences of which made themselves felt right up to the time of the unification of Italy, when Syracuse became again part of the homeland. The Syracuse of our time is a city of art and of great archaeological interest, and an outstanding tourist centre, bathing resort and centre for commercial and industrial activities. The city, especially the part on the island of Ortygia, is marked by its clean, white buildings, the beauty of its Medieval and Baroque architecture and the imposing presence of vestiges of its past. Its most typical crafts products include ceramics representing scenes of Sicilian life, wooden and leather articles and the typical objects made of papyrus, the feather in the cap of the ingenious local craftsmen. Shows include the Classical plays which are performed in the Greek Theatre every two years, and the processions with the silver statue of St. Lucia on her saint's day (13th December) and on the first Sunday in May. For those who want to go shopping, there is a daily market in Piazza Pancali which offers all kinds of clothing articles and food products (especially fruit and vegetables and fish).

ISLAND OF ORTYGIA

This charming and picturesque islet projects into the natural harbour, dividing the *Porto Grande* from the *Porto Piccolo*. The heart of Syracuse and site of the first Sicel settlements later overlaid by Corinthian colonies, it has several times acted as a refuge and bastion for the people of the entire city. In a fine setting within a fascinating landscape stand exquisite examples of Norman, Swabian, Aragonese and Catalan architecture, all of which blend with the unusual town structure that bears the early traces of the Greek peoples who lived there.

Cathedral - The Cathedral rises on the highest point in the island and has a decidedly Baroque character in the eighteenth century façade attributed to A. Palma. The *façade* overlooks a flight of steps up from the central *Piazza del Duomo* which is surrounded by other brilliant examples of Baroque architecture. The two-tiered façade is marked by powerful columns and covered in sculptures attributed to Marabitti. We will mention Saints Peter and Paul below and St. Marziano, the Virgin of the Pillar and St. Lucia in the upper tier.

On the site of the Cathedral there rose in ancient times the majestic and sumptuous *Temple of Athena*, a magnificent example of a Doric peripteral structure from the first half of the fifth century B.C. In the Byzantine age, in the seventh century A.D., the temple was transformed into a Christian basilica, as had already been done with the Temple of Concordia at Agrigento. Substantial vestiges of the temple can be seen in the fabric of the church, especially since the additions made in the Baroque age have been eliminated.

The *interior* has the characteristics of a basilica, and is divided into a nave and aisles, with a sixteenth century wooden ceiling in the nave. In the left apse is a fine Madonna of the Snow by Antonello Gagini. By the same artist is the St. Lucia in the left aisle. The beautiful Baroque altar (second half of the seventeenth century) stands out among other sixteenth to seventeenth century works in the presbytery. In the first chapel in the right aisle is a Norman baptismal font. In the second chapel, on a sarcophagus adorned with Gagini-style bas-reliefs, is a statue of St. Lucia, a seventeenth century work by P. Riaro. In the same chapel is also an eighteenth century silver frontal. The seventeenth century *Chapel of the Sacrament* is enhanced by a wrought-iron railing. The last chapel, that of the *Crucifix*, used to be adorned by fifteenth and sixteenth century canvases, including the admirable painting of St. Zosimus attributed to Antonello da Messina; but for safety reasons they have recently had to be removed.

The façade of the eighteenth century Cathedral.

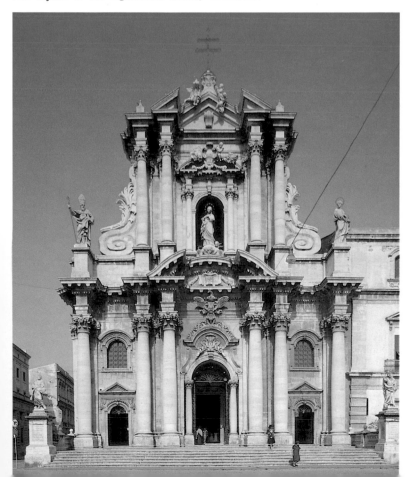

Church of Santa Lucia alla Badia - This church stands on the southern side of the Piazza del Duomo and is marked by a tall and pleasing two-tiered Baroque *façade*, the work of L. Caracciolo (seventeenth-eighteenth centuries). To both sides of the portal are spiral columns supporting architectural features which blend well with the decoration of the façade.

Church of San Martino - The present building is from the fourteenth century, but an Early Christian basilica (sixth century) stood previously on this site. The *interior* has an aisled nave defined by pilasters; there are two ancient Roman columns in the apse and a fifteenth century triptych in Gothic style.

Church of Santa Maria dei Miracoli - This church was built in the late fifteenth century; in the *façade* is a fine marble portal in Renaissance style with the typical features of the art of the Gagini. The interior has preserved some Catalan Gothic features, especially in the apse.

Church of the Collegio - This is a typically seventeenth century building of pure Baroque inspiration. It has an imposing *façade* which, however, was never completed, and the capacious interior is enhanced by a Baroque décor at its best in the admirable eighteenth century altars.

Palazzo Bellomo - Originally a Swabian building (thirteenth century), this palace has Gothic characteristics and a fine portal on the ground floor. It was rebuilt two centuries later in Catalan style; the sequence of lancet windows on the top floor is from that period. Its rooms accommodate the *Regional Gallery*.

Palazzo Arcivescovile - The Archbishop's Palace was built by Andrea Vermexio in the first half of the seventeenth century over the remains of a building from the Medieval period. The elegant façade, however, is evidence of rebuilding in the late eighteenth century; the third tier was added at that time.

Palazzo Senatorio - This Baroque building was designed by Giovanni Vermexio and built in the first half of the seventeenth century. At present used as City Hall, it is interesting from an archaeological point of view, since excavations have brought to light there vestiges of an ancient Ionian building of the sixth century B.C. identifiable as the *Temple of Artemis*.

Castello Maniace - A fortified construction of the Swabian age (thirteenth century), this castle is square in plan with cylindrical towers at the angles. Of particular interest is the splendid ogival Gothic portal, flanked by niches on which stood at one time two bronze rams. The various alterations to the building over the centuries have considerably spoilt the original beauty of the castle, especially on the ground floor, where there is still an admirable hall with pillars supporting a cross vault. It is difficult to visit the castle now since it is inside a military zone.

Fountain of Arethusa - This very ancient fresh water spring pours from a cave near the sea, in a setting made evocative by its lush vegetation and by memories associated with the works of Classical authors. Pindar and Virgil take up the tale told by Hybicus in the sixth century B.C.; already at that time he had mentioned this picturesque spring, which according to mythology is the incarnation of the story of Arethusa and Alphaeus and which has also become the symbol of the city.

A view of the Fountain of Arethusa and the remains of the Temple of Apollo.

Fountain of Artemis - This modern fountain adorns the central *Piazza Archimede*, which is surrounded by admirable buildings. The fountain is the work of Moschetti and represents in sculptural form the mythical story of Artemis and the nymph Arethusa.

Porta Marina - This gate on the sea side is the most important remaining part of the Medieval city walls, built in the fourteenth century. Above the arch is a splendidly adorned niche in Catalan style.

Temple of Apollo - At the end of *Piazza Pancali* rise the imposing ruins of this temple building, which were freed during the thirties and forties from the medieval structures that covered them. This is considered to be the oldest of the peripteral Doric temples in Sicily (sixth century B.C.), and was previously erroneously assigned to the cult of Artemis. The most substantial vestiges are those of the base and two columns; other architectural features reveal the uses the building was put to over the centuries, when it was turned into a Byzantine church, an Arab mosque and, in the Norman period, a basilica.

Regional Gallery - This interesting collection of sculptures and paintings has recently been rearranged in the rooms of the Palazzo Bellomo. The ground floor concentrates on the different phases of sculpture in Sicily from the early Christian period to the sixteenth century.
In **Room I** works of the fifth to ninth centuries (Early Christian and Byzantine sculpture) are exhibited.
Room II contains works from the Medieval period, between the twelfth and fourteenth centuries.
In **Room III** (Renaissance sculpture) we notice particularly the funerary monument of G. Cardinas, attributed to Antonello Gagini, the Madonna of the Goldfinch by Domenico Gagini and the tombstone of G. Sebastida which is reminiscent in style of Laurana.
Room IV accommodates some eighteenth century carriages.
From the Cortile della Palma (there are marble coats-of-arms there from the fifteenth to eighteenth centuries) we ascend to the first floor where the **Picture Gallery** is situated.
Room V displays panels of Byzantine inspiration and Italic or Slav origin (fifteenth-eighteenth centuries); we find also a Burial of St. Lucia by Caravaggio and a sixteenth century Russian triptych of the Strogano school, both outstanding.
The painting that stands out in **Room VI** is the Annunciation by Antonello da Messina. There is also a St. Leonard believed to be by L. Veneziano and a Madonna Enthroned with the Child and Saints by P. Serra (fourteenth century).
Room VII contains fifteenth to sixteenth century paintings; artists we should mention are Antonello da Palermo and Marco di Costanzo. There is also an admirable illuminated volume of the Flemish school (fifteenth century).
In **Room VIII** we can see sixteenth century works.
Room IX contains drawings by Filippo Paladino and paintings of the sixteenth to eighteenth centuries.
In **Rooms X** to **XIX** are exhibited interesting objects of various kinds: church jewels and vestments, furniture, embroidery, ceramics and earthenware, engravings and an eighteenth century sculpture.

THE MAINLAND AND THE ARCHAEOLOGICAL AREA

Many ruins from the Hellenistic and Roman periods can be seen in the area which used to be occupied by the ancient quarters of *Achradina* and *Tyche*. We will go on to mention the most substantial of the ruins, as well as the most important sights for tourists.

Piazza della Vittoria - Recent archaeological studies support the theory that the present square lies at what was the starting point for an important road leading to the Roman Amphitheatre and that this road formed the boundary between Achradina and Neapolis. A housing district developed along this road, on top of a zone previously occupied by necropolis.

Piazza Archimede: the Fountain of Artemis.

In this area excavations have brought to light the remains of the **Sanctuary of Demeter and Kore**, which dates from the fifth century B.C. and has yielded up a great number of votive objects. To the east of the sanctuary a **Fountain** of the fifth century B.C., which was remodelled in the third century, has been found.

Ancient Arsenal - In a fenced area near the railway have been found traces of the ancient shelters that housed the ships of the naval fleet when they were in dry dock. Studies have also made it clear that the coast of Syracuse is from the morphological point of view substantially different now from the way it appears in the descriptions of Classical authors.

Baths - In the area next to the "dockyard" the remains of a bath-house around a paved courtyard have come to light. It has several rooms, dates from the Imperial age and underwent alterations during the Byzantine period.
The theory that these baths can be identified as the place where Constans II (seventh century) was assassinated is, however, unfounded.

Forum of Syracuse - On the site now occupied by a large park with trees there once stood the Agora of the Classical city. Near the Memorial to the War Dead were found columns (some of which were placed upright again) that once belonged to a portico of the Imperial period. According to the descriptions of Cicero, this was the site of the Temple of Olympian Zeus and the Bouleuterion. From Plutarch we can deduce also the presence of a Solar Clock and the Altar of Concordia.

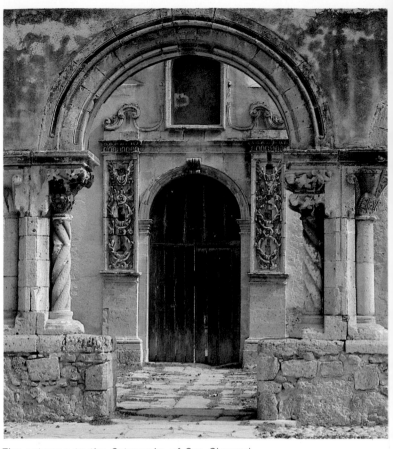

The entrance to the Catacombs of San Giovanni.

Roman Gymnasium - Excavations undertaken in the second half of the last century uncovered the remains of a building of the Roman period, improperly identified as a gymnasium. The structure, which dates from the first century A.D., was in all probability a Serapeion, at least during the first stage, before the building was completed. The most important ruins here include the raised ***Portico*** and the ***Theatre***, with a small auditorium facing the stage which also forms one side of the marble ***Temple***.

Church of Santa Lucia al Sepolcro - The original church rose in the Byzantine period, on the site where according to tradition St. Lucia was martyred. In Norman times the church was rebuilt, and of this building substantial portions remain in the apse and portal. The last alterations to the church were made in the seventeenth century.

The ***interior***, which has an aisled nave, contained interesting works of art which, however, have been transferred to the Regional Gallery . We will mention the Burial of St. Lucia, by Caravaggio, and two Crucifixes (thirteenth-fourteenth centuries).

Close by is the octagonal mass of the ***Church of the Santo Sepolcro***, a seventeenth century building by Giovanni Vermexio. Below the church extend the burrows of the ***Catacombs of St. Lucia***, built from the third century A.D. onward.

Sanctuary of the Madonna delle Lacrime - This building, circular in plan and very modern in conception, rises on the place where, in August 1953, a statue of the Virgin wept for four days, in circumstances where events believed to be miraculous occurred. The tears, which are preserved in a reliquary made by the local sculptor B. Poidimani, are an object of particular veneration for the pilgrims who come to the sanctuary from all over the world.

Catacombs of San Giovanni - This underground cemetery complex belongs to the church of the same name, which the Normans rebuilt on the site of an ancient sixth century basilica and which was ruined by the earthquake of 1693. We come first to the ***Crypt of St. Marziano***, dedicated to the first bishop of the town, who was martyred; the crypt has no aisles but three apses. The statues of the Evangelists are of the Norman period; under the northern apse is a further buried room with a fifth century fresco of the Alexandrian women praying in a garden. The system of catacombs spreading below dates from the fourth to fifth centuries.

Archaeological museum: marble statuette of Heracles, 300 B.C.

Catacombs of Vigna Cassia - This vast burial area communicates also with the *Catacombs of Santa Maria di Gesù* (third century). Along the tunnels we find arcosolium tombs, many of them decorated with frescoes; we will mention in particular the ones called of Marcia, of St. Diego and of the Roses.

Latomia dei Cappuccini - This quarry cut out of the living rock is one of the most evocative for its setting and its vegetation. Probably connected with ancient Tyche, it is believed by some writers to have been the prison of the Athenians who were defeated in 412 B.C.

Regional Archaeological Museum - Until recently housed in a building in Piazza Duomo at Ortygia, the Regional Archaeological Museum has been transferred to a very modern building in the *Park of Villa Landolina*, the site of which is a latomia containing some pagan underground tombs of the fourth century B.C. and a Protestant Cemetery where the German Romantic poet A. von Platen is buried. The collections in the museum, one of the most important in Italy from an archaeological point of view, give us a glimpse of Sicel civilization and the various colonies which followed one after another on the island from prehistoric times to the early Christian age. The following description maintains as far as possible a chronological and topographical classification, on account of the recent installation of the collections in the new and functional building.
Materials of prehistoric interest range from the Sicilian Palaeolithic (finds from Palazzolo Acreide, Pachino and Marina di Ragusa) to the Syracusan Neolithic (Megara Hyblaea, Stentinello) and the Neolithic of Paternò, to the Aeneolithic and early Bronze Age finds from Piano Notaro, Palma di Montechiaro, Castelluccio and Serrafulicchio.
The finds from the various necropolises at Syracuse and especially that of Pantalica are connected with the Bronze Age and the early Iron Age. Other finds from the same periods belong to the areas of Adrano, Mount Disueri and Agrigento (the necropolis of Sant'Angelo Muxaro).
Then follow the finds connected with the late Iron Age and the earliest Greek settlements, from Modica, ancient Noto, Lentini and Finocchito, together with materials found in the region of Enna. The Greek period begins with votive objects from the *Sanctuary of Demeter and Korè* (Terravecchia), from the excavations at Monte San Mauro near Caltagirone, from the ancient Casmene (Monte Casale) and from Akrai and Leontinoi (where grave goods have been found).
The Sicel sites which have yielded materials dating from the seventh to the third centuries B.C. include Adrano (Hadranum), Vizzini, Mineo, Morgantina and Monte San Basilio, which supplied precious tomb furnishings dating from the fourth century B.C. The finds from the city and district of Syracuse are also important; items from the sanctuaries and necropolises are shown here, mostly ceramic objects.
We should notice also the finds from the burial grounds of Gela, Megara Hyblaea, Centuripe (the admirable painted Greek vases come from this last locality) and the Greek colony of Camarina.
Bronze materials from the Archaic and Classical periods include the famous Nude Ephebus from Adrano, dating from the fifth century B.C.
There are some materials from the early Christian and Byzantine periods, mostly from the Sicel region. Architectural fragments, inscriptions and clay objects include the Telamon found at the Ara of Hiero and the Cariatid from the theatre at Syracuse. There are interesting fragments of buildings from ancient Syracusan settlements, such as the marble roof gutter with lion-head spouts and the torso of Nike (Temple of Athena), the finds from the Temple of Apollo, a Gorgon and a temple building from Gela, and clay architectural fragments from Camarina. The collection is enriched by statues from Megara Hyblaea, Syracuse and Leontinoi, and vestiges of clay decorations from the Syracusan temples of Apollo and Athena.
Sculptures worth noting include the Landolina Venus, a Roman copy of a Hellenistic original, the limestone figure of Hercules (fourth century B.C.) and a statue of the Archaic Greek period (sixth century B.C.) from Megara Hyblaea representing a Seated goddess nursing twins. There are also a Goddess enthroned, a terracotta found at Terravecchia di Grammichele, and a Torso of Athena, which was part of the fabric of a small temple at Syracuse. Examples of Greek sculpture include a marble representation of Cybeles enthroned between lions, a fine work

A view of the evocative Greek theatre.

preserved in an aedicule (fourth century B.C.), some Hellenistic steles from the latomie of Syracuse and Akrai, a small Doric aedicule and fourth century B.C. Syracusan funerary steles. Hellenistic and Roman sculpture is represented by marble figures of the Muses, found in the Mouseion of the theatre of Syracuse, figures of Pluto and Hygeia from the Asclepeion of Syracuse, and a gigantic Head of Zeus found at the amphitheatre of the same city. There are besides limestone bas-reliefs from Akrai and Messina, a head of Hercules (second century B.C.) from Centuripe, togaed statues from the Roman period and mosaic decorations of the same period from various parts of Sicily.
Among the portraits of the Hellenistic and Roman periods, those from Centuripe (Augustus, Drusus Major and Drusus Minor) are outstanding. We then find materials from the early Christian and Byzantine periods. We should notice particularly the early Christian sarcophagus found in the catacombs of San Giovanni, carved with stories from the Bible (fourth century A.D.); also interesting are the various minor finds from Hellenistic and Roman times, the funerary inscriptions of the early Christian period found in the burial grounds and catacombs of Syracuse, and some figures in togas of the Roman period found in the city's gymnasium.

Neapolis Archaeological Park - This spectacular complex of public buildings and monuments blends splendidly with the imposing quarries of the Latomie. The whole area, which has been provided with paths and is otherwise much overgrown with vegetation, is of extraordinary archaeological interest and fascinates the visitor also with its setting, the surrounding landscape and views. The zone follows in its main outlines the contours of one of the most ancient settlements in Syracuse, and can be reached by Viale Orsini, which follows an ancient Roman road, in places still visible.

Greek Theatre - This impressive theatre building, one of the largest and most evocative that have come down to us from ancient times, is built into the rocky sides of the Temenite Hill, with its auditorium toward the plain of Syracuse and its fringe of sea.
The Theatre goes back originally to the fifth century B.C., having been built by the architect Damocopos. At the time of Hiero II (third century B.C.) the structure underwent considerable remodelling and expanding, which changed its original appearance. Used both for the performance of Classical plays and for public assemblies, the Theatre was the heart

The Ara of Hiero II from the third century B.C.

of the life of Syracuse from very ancient times. Under the Romans (first to fifth centuries A.D.) the Theatre was further altered to accomodate certain kinds of plays and spectacles typical of the Roman world. Unfortunately the violent plundering of the Theatre in the first half of the sixteenth century, when the upper part of the auditorium and the stage were dismantled to be used as building material in the fortifications of Ortygia, seriously and irrevocably altered and damaged its structural integrity.

The capacious auditorium, or cavea, which once consisted of 67 tiers of seats, was reduced to 46 tiers divided into nine blocks.. In ancient times it was topped by a portico, which collapsed and of which very few vestiges remain; archaeological studies confirm the theory that the *Mouseion* which has provided valuable materials for the city's Archaeological Museum was situated there. In the central part is the *Nymphaeum*, a sort of artificial grotto from which gushed a spring of water, once part of the "plumbing" of the Theatre.

Via dei Sepolcri - On this road, dug into the rock of the Temenite Hill behind the Theatre, we can see votive niches of the Hellenistic period and Byzantine hypogea cut into the walls. Traces of the **Sanctuary of Apollo Temenites** (seventh to fourth centuries B.C.) have been found to the west of the Theatre.

Ara of Hiero II - This is the biggest altar of Greek antiquity. It was built by Hiero II in the third century B.C.and consists of a rectangular structure measuring 22.8 X 198 metres. In Roman times the the pool and portico surrounding it were added. The part cut into the rock has been preserved, while the erected walls were destroyed during the sixteenth century by the Spanish.

Roman Amphitheatre - Certainly the largest building of this kind in Sicily, the Amphitheatre dates from the first century B.C. It was built on a grand scale, largely by carving it out of the living rock. Its elliptical plan and structural affinity with the Coliseum confirm that the building was used for circuses and gladiatorial shows.

Latomie - The position, in a line, of these enormous quarries for building material, and the fact that they are situated outside the ancient Neapolis, suggest that in ancient times they were used also as defensive barriers. Dating probably from about the fifth century B.C., they certainly supplied a great quantity of building stone for the ancient city, for its houses, its public buildings and its temples. Perhaps used for holding prisoners, and even as dwelling places for the lowest classes, they continue to be one of the most distinctive and enigmatic features of the city.

Latomia del Paradiso - This is the largest and most famous of the latomie of Syracuse, reaching as far down as 45 metres. In the past it supplied enormous quantities of limestone for building purposes; it contains some interesting artificial caves.
The ***Orecchio di Dionisio*** (Ear of Dionysius), as Caravaggio called it, is in the shape of an outer ear and has extraordinary acoustic qualities. Legend recounts that the tyrant of Syracuse shut his enemies in this cave and listened to their conversations from outside.
The ***Grotta dei Cordari*** is an impressive spot and derives its name from the rope-makers ("cordari") who for a long time exercized their craft there.

Latomia dell'Intagliatella - This quarry can be reached from the previous one through a tunnel made in modern times. The place is given its charm by the citrus trees that grow there and the pillar of rock in the middle.

Latomia di Santa Venera - An arch in the rock communicates this quarry with the Latomia dell'Intagliatella. The scene here also is marked by vegetation, which is tropical in appearance. In some parts the walls are dotted with small votive niches, which have provided interesting archaeological material.

The artificial grotto called "Ear of Dionysius".

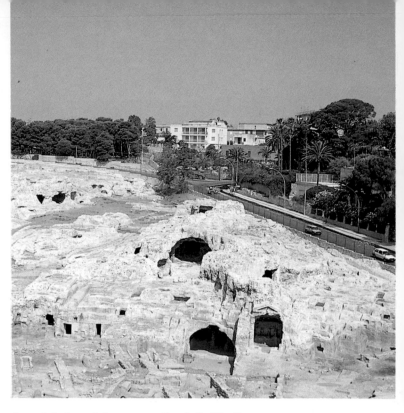

A partial view of the necropolis of Grotticelli.

Necropolis of Grotticelli - This is reached by a path from the Latomia di Santa Venera. The burial ground has yielded up graves from the Classical age and Byzantine tombs carved in the rock. Two Roman burial vaults lined with niches are particularly interesting; one of them, of monumental appearance with a fronton supported by Doric semi-columns, dates from the first century A.D. and is locally (and incorrectly) known as the *Tomb of Archimedes*.

Surroundings of the City - The *Latomia del Casale* and the *Latomia di Broggi* are situated half way between the archaeological complex of Neapolis and the Latomia dei Cappuccini. They also were exploited as quarries for building material when Neapolis was built.

The *Castle of Euryalus*, a powerful fortress, is part of a complex of buildings erected by Dionysius, which included also the walls (fourth century B.C.). The ruins as we see them today are the product of rebuilding in the Byzantine age. The castle rises on the plateau of Epipolae, at a spot considered in ancient times very vulnerable and thus a threat to the safety of Syracuse. Three wide ditches dug into the rock protected the defense bastion proper, which consisted of a trapezoidal keep in the centre with a number of towers and cisterns. An ingenious arrangement of walls hid from enemy eyes the entrance to the fortifications.

The finds from archaeological studies carried out there are exhibited in an *Antiquarium*. Particularly interesting are a bas-relief with a picture of a catapult, the remains of a Greek inscription and two lion-head spouts which belonged to the towers of the keep.

The *Ciane Spring*, also known as Testa della Pisma, can be reached by boat up the Ciane river, picturesque with its lush, spontaneous growth of papyrus reeds, which unfortunately are suffering from the pollution of the environment. The Ciane Spring consists of a round basin where the river is born, connected in mythology with the story of Pluto.

A little before the spring, on the right bank of the river, rise the ruins of the *Olympeion*, the sanctuary dedicated to the cult of Olympian Zeus (Jove or Jupiter). All that is still visible of this ancient building, founded in the sixth century B.C., is the base and two columns still standing on the south side.

AUGUSTA

This small town spreads along an island connected by bridges to the mainland, in the upper part of the Gulf of Augusta.

The name goes back to the Roman Imperial age, when Augustus founded a new colony here (first century B.C.). Up to two centuries earlier, the Greek colony of *Megara Hyblaea* had existed in this area, but was devastated in conflicts with the Syracusans and Romans.

Augusta itself was razed by the Saracens and rebuilt by the Swabians (thirteenth century). Subsequently an Aragonese possession, it suffered badly in more recent times, during the seventeenth and nineteenth centuries, from earthquakes.

The locality is also known for an Allied landing there during the last World War (July 1943).

A centre of the oil and petrochemical industry, it possesses refineries, factories and a busy commercial port.

The *Castle* goes back to the Swabian period (thirteenth century) and has been used as a prison.

The *Duomo*, originally built in the seventeenth century, had to be rebuilt as a result of the earthquake of 1693 and was completed in the second half of the eighteenth century.

A detail of the ruins of Megara Hyblaea, a Greek colony founded in the eighth century B.C.

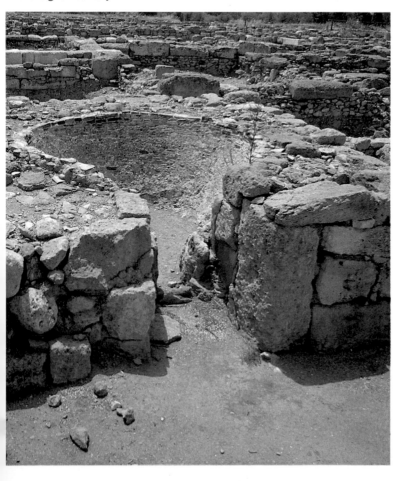

The **Palazzo Comunale** is an elegant seventeenth century building. The Baroque **Church of the Anime Purganti** (seventeenth century) is also interesting.

The sixteenth century fortalices of **Avalos**, **Garzia** and **Victoria** can still be seen at the port.

We recommend the excursion to the **ruins of Megara Hyblaea**, which was one of the most ancient Greek colonies in Sicily. The city was founded by Megara (eighth century B.C.) and flourished until its complete destruction by Roman militia under the command of Marcellus (213 B.C.) It is not easy to understand the layout of the city as restored to us by excavation, since a Hellenistic city was superimposed on an earlier archaic settlement.

An **Antiquarium** exhibits some finds from archaeological studies, but the greater part of the material has been transferred to the museum in the capital.

The ruins easiest to identify include the remains of the **ring walls**, which belong the the Hellenistic period, and the ruins of two turreted structures. The **agora** has been identified; it is surrounded by vestiges of houses of the Hellenistic period, with shops and a courtyard that must have had a wooden colonnade. We can see also traces of very ancient houses, dating from the eighth century B.C. In the upper part of the agora, the point where the **Stoa** (seventh century B.C.) stood has been identified. There are also interesting remains of a **Sanctuary** of the Hellenistic period, of a **Doric temple** probably dedicated to the cult of Aphrodite (fourth century B.C.), of a **Gymnasium** and other temple buildings.

Finally, we should notice the remains of a large **house** of the Hellenistic period, where it is still possible to make out the division of the rooms, and those of a structure used as a bath-house, with a primitive heating system, later converted by the Romans into a lime kiln.

PALAZZOLO ACREIDE

An important archaeological centre, this town lies up against the spurs of the Hyblaean Hills, in the upper Anapo valley. The modern town was founded in the eighteenth century, near the place where once rose the ancient Syracusan colony of *Akrai*, settled in the seventh century B.C. Akrai belonged almost always to the sphere of its settlers, unhappy under Roman imperialism. Destroyed a first time by the Arabs (ninth century), it was rebuilt by the Normans who called it Palazzolo. Again ruined by the earthquake of 1693, it was rebuilt soon afterwards on its present site.

The **Church of San Pietro e Paolo** (eighteenth century) has a turreted and highly ornate façade, attributed to the architect V.Sinatra.

The seventeenth century **Church of San Sebastiano** has an elaborate façade in Baroque style overlooking a magnificent flight of steps. Opposite it stands the **Palazzo del Municipio** (City Hall), a last century building with porticoes.

In the Church of the Immacolata we can see a fine sculpture by F.Laurana representing the Virgin and Child. Ethnographical samples and information are preserved in the House and Museum of Antonino Uccello. On the slopes of the nearby **Acremonte Hill** spread the numerous ruins of the **Archaeological Zone**. The main roads going through them, which divide them into somewhat irregular blocks, probably date from the late Hellenistic period.

The **Theatre**, discovered in the first half of the last century, was built in the third century B.C., and although small is fairly well preserved, except where it was despoiled, during the reconstruction of Palazzolo in the eighteenth century, for building material. The auditorium (partially rebuilt) has twelve tiers of seats in nine blocks.

The **Bouleuterion** stands close by, at the agora, and has six tiers of seats in a semi-circle. The senate of the city used to meet here.

The remains of an archaic temple building (sixth century B.C.) on the site on the **acropolis** provide evidence that a **Temple of Aphrodite** once stood there.

On the south-east slopes of the hill are two stone quarries. The **Latomia dell'Intagliatella** has small niches where little votive panels could have been placed, and a bas-relief carved in the rock with scenes of sacrifices and a banquet. In the nearby Latomia dell'Intagliata, hypogea and catacombs of the early Christian period and cave dwellings from Byzantine times have been found. The **"Templi Ferali"** are in fact a latomia of similar appearance to the above, where votive and sacrificial objects have been found.

On the the eastern slopes of the Acremonte are the **"Santoni"**, strange rock carvings of the third century B.C. which spread along a wall of rock and can be connected with the cult of Cybeles.

It is worthwhile making a trip to the Necropolis of Pantalica. It was here that the Sicel settlement of Hybla stood in ancient times. The impressive ruins of the burial ground are some of the biggest in the island, consisting of an astonishing number of cave tombs excavated in the rock. Many of these gave rise in Byzantine and Medieval times to communities of cave dwellers. The remains of the megalithic **Anaktoron** (Princes' Palace) dating from the twelfth to eleventh century B.C. stand out among the ruins.

The Intagliatella, a stone quarry of the Greek period with rock reliefs.

NOTO

Noto is a large town in the province of Syracuse which spreads over a terraced slope at the lower edge of the Hyblaean Hills, overlooking the sea.

The present town is of markedly eighteenth century character, with a regular grid layout. It can in fact be said to originate in the eighteenth century, having been completely rebuilt at that time, in a place believed to be safe, after the disastrous earthquake of 1693 had razed the previous town, which was situated higher up, to the north-west. The ancient town was founded by the Sicanians and was known as *Neetum*; colonized by the Greeks and later taken by the Syracusans and the Romans, it became *Capovalle* on the coming of the Arabs and went through a period of flourishing development which continued right through the sixteenth century. Devastated by the earthquake and rebuilt, with the unification of Italy it lost its administrative privileges in favour of Syracuse. Its most characteristic folk festivities include the Processione della Santa Spina (Procession of the Holy Thorn), which is held on Good Friday, and the Cili di San Corrado, a procession of people in costume carrying giant candles when the patron saint of the town is taken out into the streets.

The **Duomo** is dedicated to San Nicolò and overlooks an imposing flight of steps. The façade is harmonious and elegant, on two tiers, divided vertically by columns and flanked by twin bell towers. The bronze portal,

Palazzo Ducezio, the town hall (eighteenth century); opposite, a detail of Palazzo Villadorata.

which shows episodes from the life of *St. Nicholas*, is a contemporary work by G.F. Pirrone. The interior has an aisled nave and splendid marble decorations. On the right side of the transept, in a chapel, is the precious silver urn with the remains of St. Corrado Confalonieri (sixteenth century).

The Basilica of the Santissimo Salvatore is marked by its fine façade in pure Neo-Classical style.

The eighteenth century **Palazzo Ducezio** (the City Hall) was designed by V. Sinatra and has an artistic loggia in front of it.

The **Church of San Domenico**, adjacent to the ex-monastery, was built by the Gagliardi and is characterized by the curvilinear forms of its Baroque façade, which is adorned by slim columns.

The elegant Palazzo San Alfano (nineteenth century) has a façade on three tiers, divided by pilasters.

The Church of San Francesco (eighteenth century) looks down on a flight of steps and has fine architectural qualities.

The Church of the Crocifisso is a building from the seventeenth to eighteenth centuries; the façade, however, was never completed. It has a fine portal flanked by pillar-bearing lions in Romanesque style. Inside, on the right side of the transept is a fine statue of the Virgin attributed to Laurana.

The City Museum exhibits archaeological finds from prehistoric times, the Greek age (in particular ceramic and clay materials of the sixth to third centuries B.C. found in a Sanctuary of Demeter and Kore), and medieval materials from ancient Noto and from the Abbey of Santa Lucia del Mendolo (Norman period). A modern art section has recently been added. An excursion to the ruins of Ancient Noto will allow us to the see the remains of the walls and castle and the so-called Porta Reale (Royal Gate).

The Baroque Church of San Domenico.

CATANIA

Historical Note - The city spreads along the upper edge of the gulf of the same name, on the Ionian coast of Sicily, in an extremely beautiful natural setting. The mountain of Etna, with its perpetual white cloak of snow, forms a natural backdrop to the city and contrasts strongly with the intense blue of the sky and the yellow of the citrus groves.

The Chalcidian colony of *Catinon* was superimposed on extremely ancient previous settlements, existing in the place since prehistoric times. Subsequently a possession of Gelon of Syracuse who called it *Aetna*, it fell again into the hands of its founders (461 B.C.) and was given back its original name. In following centuries the city underwent various vicissitudes connected with the unstable, constantly changing political situation in Sicily at that time.

In the second half of the third century B.C. the Romans made it first a *civitas decumana* and then a true colony, assuring it a period of relative tranquillity. At the time of the persecutions of the Christians, Catania gave birth to St.Agatha, an acclaimed martyr and the present patron saint of the city. From the sixth century on it was subjected by Ostrogoths and Byzantines, who were followed by the Arabs. In the eleventh century it passed into the hands of the Normans, who undertook the construction of buildings such as the Cathedral. It was then the turn of the Swabians, followed by the Aragonese, who built the Castello Ursino and made Catania their favourite place of residence. The fortunes of the city improved during the long years spent under Spanish dominion, even though the same years heralded sorrow and devastation from recurrent famines and plagues, and from the earthquakes that profoundly altered the fabric of the city in the second half of the seventeenth century. In 1669 a devastating eruption of Etna covered the city with a thick layer of lava, which reached as far as the sea. Not even thirty years later, in 1693, a catastrophic earthquake completed the ruinous effect of the volcano; the city had to be rebuilt once more, and rose this time with the Baroque character that has lasted up to the present, according to the designs of G.B.Vaccarini who carried out faithfully the wishes of the Duke of Camastra.

In the nineteenth century Catania took a leading part in the Risorgimento struggles that culminated in the rebellion of Garibaldi. Seriously damaged during the Second World War, the Catania of our days is substantially modern and dynamic in appearance and preserves abundant evidence of its Baroque restoration in the eighteenth century.

The city has a fortunate situation, in a district of increasing importance in the tourist trade, not far from well known resorts on the coast and

Panorama of the town with the eighteenth century Cathedral.

the volcano of Etna, which besides its interest as a natural phenomenon is acquiring increasing importance as a centre for winter sports and hiking; it also possesses a very active port and is equipped for extensive and diversified commercial, industrial and service activities, to the extent that it may be considered a rival of the regional capital, Palermo.

Its most characteristic festivities include the popular Festival of St.Agatha, in February, when huge candles made of gilt wood are carried in procession. One of the most typical features of the festivities, which last for several days, is a procession of the devotees of the Saint dressed in white clothes.

The place where the people of Catania meet and take their evening stroll is the central Via Etnea, which is the main shopping centre and where the delicious cakes and pastries of the city, similar to those of other parts of the island, can be tasted. The picturesque and colourful fish market, a typical feature of the customs of Sicily, is held every morning near the Duomo. A lively fruit and vegetable market is held in Piazza Carlo Alberto; it is possible to buy there produce brought directly from their fields by the farmers. In Piazza del Carmine is held the traditional Fiera del Lunedì (Monday Fair), a sort of folk flea-market. In the university area it is possible to buy antique goods from the loud-voiced dealers. Some of the most typical Catanese crafts we should mention are wrought-iron objects, bronze sculptures of stylized animals, embroidery, musical instruments (guitars, lutes and mandolins), marauni (Jew's harps), jewellery and necklaces in amber and lava stone, and finally the ubiquitous puppets.

Duomo - The Cathedral faces the Piazza Duomo, which provides a refined and harmonious setting. The building was founded in the time of the Norman king Roger I, in the last decade of the eleventh century. Of that original building the back part with three apses and a portion of the transept remain. As early as 1169 a serious earthquake brought down a large part of the Norman structure, which was then rebuilt and again razed by the devastating earthquake of 1693.

The subsequent rebuilding brought into being the Cathedral as we see it today, according to the design of Fra Girolamo Palazzotto which was later completed by the admirable *façade* by G.B.Vaccarini. This façade is one of the masterpieces of the Baroque style in Sicily; it was built in the first half of the eighteenth century and has two tiers of columns, of which those on the ground floor are very ancient and probably belonged to an earlier building. We should notice the niche high on the façade adorned with a statue of *St.Agatha and the Angel*.

The imposing *interior*, which is divided into a nave and two aisles, offers us an exceptionally fascinating ambience, deriving from the combination of elements of the original Norman architecture with the Baroque reconstruction superimposed on them. The transept, which survives from the first Norman building, has at its ends two incomplete bell towers, while over its centre rises the cupola of Battaglia. By the second pilaster on the right is the *tomb of Vincenzo Bellini* (1810-1835), one of the most illustrious sons of the city; it has a bas-relief representing the heroines from the operas of the famous composer.

In the right transept, through a sixteenth century portal by G.B.Mazzola, we reach the **Chapel of the Madonna**, on the altar of which is a six-

Piazza del Duomo: the Cathedral and the Fountain of the Elephant.

The magnificent Castello Ursino, thirteenth century.

teenth century statue of the Virgin. In the same chapel are a Roman sarcophagus (third century), which contains the remains of princes of the
House of Aragon, and a similar sarcophagus of Medieval date containing
the body of Constance of Aragon.
In the right apse is the **Chapel of St.Agatha**, which is enclosed by an
exquisite wrought-iron railing. We can admire there the *Funerary monument of the Viceroy Ferdinando d'Acuña*, a very fine work by the sculptor
Antonello Freri of Messina, a contemporary of Gagini. Also by Freri are
the marble bas-relief representing St.Agatha among the Saints and Evangelists and the carved portal which leads to the Treasury of St.Agatha.
The Treasury, which contains very interesting valuables, is accessible to
the public only on days when the patron saint of Catania is commemorat-
ed. The presbytery accommodates an admirable wooden choir carved
with Scenes of the life of St.Agatha, the work of Scipione di Guido (second half of the sixteenth century).
In the left transept, through a sixteenth century portal by Mazzola, we
reach the Chapel of the Crucifix, where we can see sections of the original medieval building.
In the Sacristy, we should notice a fine seventeenth century fresco by
G.Platania representing the devastating Eruption of Etna in 1669. In the
structures of the Duomo and the nearby Seminario dei Chierici (eighteenth century), as well as under the square, the remains have been identified of ancient thermal installations of the Roman period, known as the
Terme di Achille (Baths of Achilles).

Badia di Sant'Agata - This picturesque eighteenth century church looks
on to the side of the Duomo (from Via Vittorio Emanuele II), and is a
fine work by the architect Vaccarini. The building is marked by its imposing cupola and the curvilinear grace of its rich façade, which is reminiscent of the style favoured by Borromini.
On the same street, on the other side a little beyond the Duomo, is the
imposing **Church of San Placido**, built in the second half of the eighteenth century.

Church of San Nicolò - This eighteenth century church is one of the
largest religious buildings in Sicily, and is characterized by its powerful
façade, which remained incomplete and is adorned with immense truncated columns. Especially striking is the crowning of the central portion

of the façade, which is of dark lava rock that contrasts with the clean white of the wall.

The *interior*, of imposing dimensions, is divided into a nave and aisles by impressive pillars, and is marked by sober lines and the complete absence of decorative features. In the floor of the transept is a curious *sundial* with the signs of the zodiac, the work of Bertel Thorwaldsen (first half of the nineteenth century). Over the altars are paintings of the seventeenth to nineteenth centuries. In the presbytery we notice an admirable eighteenth century *organ* by D.del Piano, and a fine choir in carved wood.

In the left transept is the entrance to the *Cappella dei Caduti* (Chapel of the War Dead) and the *Sacristy*, which has the characteristics of the Rococo style and where we can see valuable vestments and paraments as well as rich furniture of the period. The adjacent Benedictine Monastery is marked by imposing architectural features and eighteenth century ornamental motifs.

Church of San Giuliano - This Baroque building is also the work of G.B Vaccarini, who completed it in the second half of the eighteenth century. The *façade* has curvilinear forms and an arcade. The interior has an unusual octagonal plan and is topped by a cupola. Worth noting is the richly ornamented high altar, which has on it a fine fifteenth century Crucifix.

Church of the Jesuits - This is an eighteenth century building, known also as the Church of Sant'Ignazio. The *façade*, of the same date, is the work of A.Italia and is marked by two tiers of twin columns.

Immediately adjacent is the eighteenth century *Church of San Benedetto*, the distinctive features of which are the fine, richly ornamented *façade* and the ornate interior with its single nave, reached through a vestibule which is also adorned with sculptures in stucco.

Church of San Francesco d'Assisi - This building has an admirable *façade* with marked Baroque traits. The most artistically valuable feature of the *interior* is a polychrome wooden statue of the Immaculate Virgin, an eighteenth century work which stands in a niche on the inside of the façade.

Church of the Santo Carcere - The name of this church derives from the fact that in Roman times a jail ("carcere") in which St.Agatha was imprisoned stood on this site. The present building was erected on the remains of some Spanish fortifications which were later raised here. The impressive *façade* is enhanced by a Romanesque portal of the thirteenth century, which was earlier on the façade of the Duomo and was transferred to its present place in 1750.

Piazza Stesicoro: the remains of the Roman amphitheatre.

Church of Santa Maria di Gesù - Founded in the fifteenth to sixteenth centuries, this church was rebuilt in the first decade of the eighteenth century and substantially remodelled in the first half of the last century. The **Cappella Paternò**, which can be seen at the left of the façade, was part of the original building; it is marked by a brown lunette of the school of Gagini. This chapel can be reached from inside the church by way of a marble portal with a Pietà by A.Gagini (first half of the sixteenth century) and is marked by Gothic features; over the altar is a sixteenth century painting. On the second altar to the left is a Madonna and Child also by A.Gagini, while the Crucifix on the high altar is the work of Fra Umile da Petralia.

Porta Garibaldi (Garibaldi Gate) - This monumental Baroque structure was raised in 1768 to commemorate an anniversary of the royal wedding between Ferdinando III of Sicily and Maria Carolina of Austria. Built of dark lava rock and white limestone, it presents an unusual contrast in colours. The ornamental motifs above the fornix are in pure Baroque style.

Porta Uzeda - This structure from the end of the seventeenth century, Baroque in appearance, stands at the beginning of the *Via Etnea*, the lively centre of the city, its main street, lined with architecturally fine buildings, and the meeting place of the citizens of Catania.
Close by, overlooking the port, is the **Palazzo dell'Arcivescovado** (Archbishop's Palace), with the **Palazzo Biscari** a little further on. These buildings, attributed to the architect A.Amato, are typical examples of Baroque architecture.

Palazzo del Municipio - The City Hall faces the *Piazza del Duomo* where we can see the **Fountain of the Elephant**, an eighteenth century work by G.B.Vaccarini who composed it by standing an Egyptian obelisk on an ancient elephant in lava rock, probably from the Roman period: this image has become the emblem of the city of Catania. Known in popular idiom as *Liotru*, it is of Carthaginian origin according to some sources and Byzantine according to others, and was restored by Vaccarini himself after being damaged in the earthquake of 1693.
The **Palazzo del Municipio** was built by Vaccarini in the first half of the eighteenth century and is marked by admirable architectural forms. We should observe the ashlar-work on the ground floor, the arrangement of the pilasters, the balconied windows on the upper floor, and the central portal flanked by twin columns which support the balustrade of the middle balcony.

Castello Ursino - This powerful square castle was built in the first half of the thirteenth century by Riccardo da Lentini, who designed it for Frederick II of Swabia. The king wanted it to defend his coastline from the danger of pirate raids as well as to provide him with a fortress in the city from which he could control possible popular insurrections. The castle was remodelled in the sixteenth century and restored after the damage it suffered in the eruption of Etna in 1669. The last time it was restored was in the first half of this century. The complex has ramparts and is surrounded by a moat, with cylindrical towers at the ends and smaller turreted structures in the middle of each side. The rooms in the castle house an interesting museum.

Roman Theatre - The easily recognizable remains of this Roman theatre building go back to the Imperial period, when it was erected on the site of an ancient Greek theatre of the fifth century B.C. It is reached by way of the door to the building of the *Soprintendenza alle Belle Arti* (Via Vittorio Emanuele 266). We can admire the central portion of the auditorium, the ambulatories and the remains of the orchestra with its marble floor.
Immediately adjacent are the remains of the **Odeon**, a sort of smaller theatre where the members of the chorus rehearsed.

Roman amphitheatre - The amphitheatre stands at the edge of Piazza Stesicoro, and is an important example of Roman public building. The imposing elliptical structure was only slightly smaller than the Coliseum *eatro Bellini, opened in 1890.*

n Rome. It dates from the second century A.D.; it seems it was able to eat up to 16,000 spectators. Decaying and ruined from the fifth century onward, it became a quarry for materials for new public works. On the square, at the end of which stands the façade of the **Church of he Cappuccini**, we find also the **Monument to Bellini** erected in the econd half of the last century by G. Monteverde.

Palazzo San Giuliano - This eighteenth century building stands on Piaz-a dell'Università, which forms an important architectural complex lesigned by Vaccarini in the eighteenth century and including also the back of the Palazzo Municipale and the **Palazzo dell'Università**, which s of the same date and possesses an admirable inner courtyard.

Teatro Bellini - This theatre is a building in Classical style of the second nalf of the last century, named after the great composer from Catania. t is the work of the architects A. Scala and C. Sada, and is distinguished by its splendid auditorium.

Villa Bellini - This park is the lung of the city, a green space with flourishing vegetation that includes many samples of rare and exotic plant and tree species. Along its avenues we distinguish busts of impor-ant people. From two small hills inside the limits of the park we can admire fine views.

Palazzo delle Scienze (Palace of Sciences) - This modern building ac-commodates the departments of some university institutes with their museums. Those of Vulcanology, Geology and Mineralogy are of extreme nterest to natural scientists.

City Museum - The principal museum of Catania is housed in the rooms of the Castello Ursino and is of great archaeological and artistic interest. n the **Courtyard** are materials found in the city: an inscription from the aqueduct, sarcophagi in lava rock from the Roman period and fragments of an ancient obelisk.

Bellini Museum - The house where Vincenzo Bellini was born is now a museum. We can study there mementoes and information on the life and work of the great composer from Catania.

117

Panorama of the coast of Aci Castello.

ACI CASTELLO - ACI TREZZA

Aci Castello is the first important centre on the picturesque *Riviera dei Ciclopi*, which lies to the north of Catania and the population of which has lived for centuries by fishing, using even now their traditional methods. In relatively recent times the locality has undergone considerable development as a summer bathing and holiday resort, while in the surrounding countryside intensive citrus cultivation prospers. In the second half of the twelfth century the town was razed by a disastrous earthquake, which forced the population to take refuge in neighbouring localities; developing as centres, these places preserved in their names the recognizable prefix "Aci".

The distinctive feature of Aci Castello is, precisely, the **Castle**; founded by the Normans and built on top of a dark basalt rock in the second half of the eleventh century; it is memorable for its situation sheer above the sea.

The nearby town of **Aci Trezza** is known as the scene of the events in Giovanni Verga's famous novel *I Malavoglia*. It is also a popular bathing resort in a very charming natural setting. A few hundred metres from the shore the basalt shapes of the **faraglioni** or "Scogli dei Ciclopi" (Rocks of the Cyclops) rise from the sea; according to tradition, these rocks are the huge stones that the giant Polyphemus threw at Ulysses. The largest of these rocks, once known as the *Island of Lachea*, was donated by a private citizen to the University of Catania, which has installed there a marine physics and biology research station.

A view of the rocks of Aci Trezza.

Piazza del Duomo: the eighteenth century Cathedral.

ACIREALE

This town stands on a terraced slope of volcanic origin between the last spurs of Etna and the Ionian coast. Its fame comes from its thermal springs, also of volcanic origin, which have given rise to modern spas. The natural setting of the town is marked by extensive citrus plantations; it has a flourishing economy based on trade and crafts with a certain amount of industry.

The *Terme di S. Venera* spa is set in a pleasant park. There are several hotels offering hypothermal therapy using sulphureous spring waters of volcanic origin. Its waters, which contain salt, bromine and iodine, are also used in mud therapy, and are helpful in the treatment of arthropathies, arthrites and polyarthrites, in the after-effects of traumas, in skin diseases, and in gynecological, respiratory and ear-nose-and-throat diseases.

The *Duomo* dates from the sixteenth to seventeenth centuries, but was remodelled in the eighteenth century. The seventeenth century façade is the work of G.B.Basile and is marked by a fine portal in marble alabaster (seventeenth century). The majestic interior has its crossing and choir richly decorated in frescoes, the work of eighteenth century artists (P.P.Vasta, A.Filocamo). The frescoes in the vault of the nave are from the beginning of this century (by G. Sciuti). There is an admirable silver image of St. Venera, the patron saint of the town, kept in the chapel of the same name in the right transept; it was made around the middle of the seventeenth century by M.d'Angelo. We should observe a sundial from the first half of the last century in the floor of the transept.

*The Basilica of San Pietro e Paolo and the Baroque Church
of San Sebastiano.*

In the Piazza del Duomo, the centre of the town, we find also the **Palazzo Comunale**, of the second half of the seventeenth century, in typical Catanese Baroque style, and the **Basilica of Santi Pietro e Paolo**, a seventeenth century building with the characteristics of a basilica, the distinguishing features of which are the lively lines of the façade, a splendid piece of architecture on two tiers crowned by ornaments; the elegant columns that divide up its space are of twin design on the inside. There is a very fine adjacent bell tower topped by a powerfully ascending spire and decorated in the middle with lancet windows.

The **Palazzo Pennisi di Fioristella** houses an interesting numismatic collection with rare items from the Greco-Siculan period (6th-4th century B.C.). In the **Accademia Zalantea** is an important collection of paintings from the 17th-18th centuries as well as sculptures and archaeological finds; the *Bust of Julius Caesar* is particularly interesting.

The **Church of San Sebastiano** is an elaborate Baroque construction of the 17th century; the façade is richly decorated with sculptural and ornamental elements. The balustrade surmounted by statues is a later addition (18th century). The interior has three naves and is decorated with 18th century frescoes by the local artist P.P. Vasta, including a fine *San Sebastiano nursed by holy women.*

The spa complex of San Venera, whose waters are of vulcanic origin.

RANDAZZO

This town is situated near the meeting of the Alcantara and Flascio rivers, in the valley between the volcanic massif of Etna and the Nebrodi-Peloritani mountain chain. The layout of the town reveals its medieval origin; it has many buildings in volcanic stone, and goes back to the Byzantine period, having grown up on the site of an ancient Sicel settlement. It prospered particularly under the Aragonese. The locality has undergone some development as a winter resort, and is known for the Processione della Vara, which is held during the August holidays and involves the use of a huge cart carrying children.

The **Church of San Nicolò** is of fourteenth century origin; the fabric of the apse is of that period. The building as we see it today is the result of alterations in the sixteenth and seventeenth centuries; it contains important sculptures by Gagini, including a St.Nicholas and (in the transept) some Scenes of Christ's Passion. The most interesting painting is a Virgin with Saints by artists from Messina (fifteenth century).

The **Church of Santa Maria** is from the thirteenth century; the original

The Gothic façade of the Church of Santa Maria.

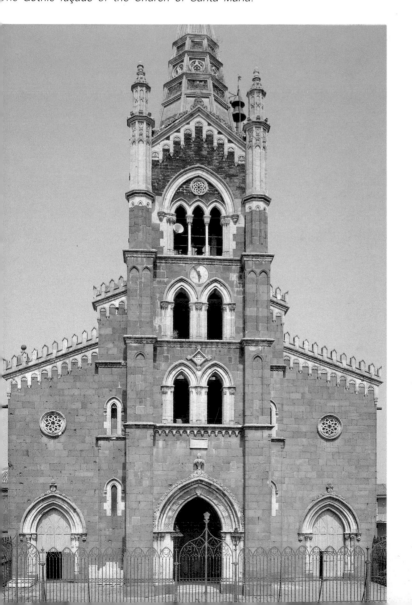

three apses of the building still stand. The portals at the sides possess fifteenth century Catalan features, while the façade and the bell tower, in their final version, date from alterations made in the second half of the last century. The interior has an aisled nave and is adorned by sixteenth to eighteenth century paintings and sculptures from the workshop of the Gagini, including a polygonal shrine and the baptismal font.

The **Church of San Martino** has a distinctive fourteenth century bell tower, in which limestone alternates with lava rock, creating an admirable effect. Inside, in the smaller right apse, is a painting of the school of Messina representing the Virgin and Child with Saints, and a wooden Crucifix dating from the first half of the sixteenth century. The baptismal font is of marble, from the first half of the fifteenth century, while there is a Virgin of Mercy, in the style of Gagini, in the right aisle.

Near the church is an interesting **tower-house**, a medieval structure once used as a prison.

The **Palazzo Finocchiaro** is from the sixteenth century; its distinctive features are the façade adorned with lancet windows and the Latin inscription on the cornice.

The **Palazzo Reale** was built in the thirteenth to fourteenth centuries, but has come down to us in a very poor state of repair.

The **Alcàntara gorge**, an absolute must for tourists visiting the area, can be reached from Taormina-Giardini Naxos by following the main road inland (185) towards Francavilla di Sicilia for 13 kilometres. This natural monument of basalt rock was created by the eruption of the *volcano Monte Moio*, Etna's most eccentric offshoot, around the year 2400 BC. The lava flow invaded the entire valley of the Alcàntara river as far as its mouth on the coast, where the Greeks founded their first colony in Sicily.

In the Sciara Larderia region the river of lava reached a thickness of 70 metres. While still white-hot, and due to a telluric settling, a sinuous longitudinal crack opened in the lava over a length of 500 metres, 70 metres deep and five metres wide, thus assuming the structure of a gorge. Only later, all the waters of the catchment basin feeding the Alcàntara river flowed into the fissure and from this derived the name "Alcàntara gorge". The continuous action of the water smoothed the basalt walls of the gorge producing that gleaming lustre which can be admired only under the action of light.

The gorge is reached by way of a scenic footpath or by means of modern elevators. To reach the entrance of the gorge the use of wading boots is recommended, which can be hired at the site; these are a useful protection against the icy water and spiky rocks. The gorge is always a dangerous place for non-experts and those who are unfamiliar with the site.

There is a large car-park, a bar, a restaurant and farm holiday facilities; it is possible to stay the night, and taste and buy excellent food prepared with traditional recipes.

The basalt gorges of the Alcantara, the product of river erosion.

Etna: eruption and lava flow at night. On the following pages: other pictures of the fascinating vulcanic landscape.

ETNA AND THE SURROUNDING AREA

Mount Etna, which is 3343 metres high, is the tallest active volcano in the continent of Europe. Because of its great importance to the natural sciences, its exceptionally beautiful landscape and its human and ecological interest, the Etna district has recently been declared, with the proper legislative backing of the Region of Sicily, a National Park.

Very interesting for hikers and sight-seers, Mount Etna cannot be missed by visitors to the island or anyone who wants to witness personally the spectacular attraction of its volcanic activity, which continues almost without interruption and occasionally reaches peaks of overwhelming intensity. The highest part of the volcano has also attracted tourists interested in snow sports, and adequate facilities for the practice of the most popular winter sports have been provided. This imposing volcanic mass, whose huge cone dominates the north-eastern section of the island, has since very ancient times played an active part in the island's life and been surrounded by myths and legends. Known also as *Mongibello*, a name of ancient Arab origin, it is marked by the great variety of species of trees and plants that clothe its sides and change as its altitude increases, making way finally for a landscape of desert character. The many eruptions which have occurred over the centuries have often altered the profile of Etna, forming new vents, pushing up new cones, and profoundly altering also the contours of the local orographic structure and its morphological features.

Of the innumerable eruptions that have occurred (at least 135 have been counted in historical times), one of the most disastrous was that of 1669, which had terrible consequences for nearby Catania. In this century there have been frequent eruptions, some of which have been extremely serious and caused considerable damage and waste in the Etna district. One of the most recent and spectacular eruptions, in Spring 1983, made it necessary to use explosives to deviate in a safe direction the immense streams of lava which were threatening villages on the slopes of the volcano.

One of the classical itineraries for a visit to the volcano branches off at Catania on the **Nicolosi** road as far as the Cantoniera dell'Etna; from here it is possible to visit the spectacular crater, with the help of expert guides and carefully respecting elementary rules of caution and common sense. The top of the crater can be extremely dangerous, because the volcano may throw up pyroclastic material, sometimes unexpectedly.

A trip particularly worth taking uses as a base the **Sapienza Refuge** (1910 metres), which makes it possible to walk right round the volcano, passing by interesting villages and admiring one of the most distinctive landscapes in Sicily. The same route can be covered by bus or by the railway that runs round the mountain. **Trecastagni**, a small village which serves also as a holiday resort, lies on the south-eastern slopes of Etna and has a fine view of Catania and the coast. The **Chiesa Madre** is interesting; it is in Renaissance style and is believed to be the work of A. Gagini.

In the **Sanctuary of San Alfio** is preserved an interesting collection of ex-votos. It is a tradition for pilgrims and the people of Catania to visit it every year on the saint's day.

Lido di Plaia spreads along the coast to the south of Catania, being the city's best known and most frequented bathing resort. The services available are excellent; the beach is sandy and surrounded by pines.

A typical lavic cave.

MESSINA

Historical Note - This city, known as the *Gateway to Sicily* lies under the foothills of the Peloritani mountains, facing the strait of Messina, which takes its name from the city and is the umbilical cord joining Sicily to the continent. Called **Zancle** by the natives of the island because of the sickle shape of its natural harbour, it was settled by Chalcidian peoples as far back as the eighth century B.C. Later a possession of Anaxilas of Rhegium, it was populated by Messenian colonists who gave it the name of *Messana*. In the centuries that followed, the city was the cause of fierce disputes betwen Doric and Ionian peoples, and was involved in the conflicts betwcen the Sicilian cities which culminated in the victory of Hannibal and the Carthaginian occupation. In 264 B.C. the Romans intervened, freeing the city from the Carthaginians and making it into a bridgehead for further conquests in the island. The new *civitas foederata* then enjoyed a long period of prosperity and well-being, forming a sort of "happy island" in the midst of the troubled scene presented by the rest of Sicily, which suffered plundering, death and devastation under Verres and in the war of the slaves.

After the fall of the empire the city was occupied by Goths and Byzantines, who held it for a long time, up until the coming of the Muslims (ninth century). In the eleventh century the city, which was deeply catholic at heart and impatient under Arab rule, welcomed the Norman invaders, who made it into an important local capital. Subsequently subjected to Swabian rule, it could not tolerate the loss of its independence, which gave rise to an impulsive revolt (first half of the thirteenth century). Messina was then taken over by the Angevins (except that it fought them at the time of the "Vespers"); becoming Aragonese, it followed the fortunes of the Spanish house, although with brief interruptions, until the eighteenth century. On the coming of the Savoys, Bourbons and Austrians during the first three decades of the eighteenth century, it fell into the sphere of the Bourbons (1734), who ruled it until Sicily was annexed to the Kingdom of Italy in 1860.

The city lies in an area with a very high earthquake risk, and has often been scourged by earthquakes. Among those in relatively recent times we will mention the one on February 5th 1783, which razed it to the ground, and the catastrophic one on 18th December 1908, which was followed by a tidal wave and almost wiped Messina from the face of the earth at dawn of that day, claiming not less than 80,000 victims in the

Piazza del Duomo: aerial view of the Cathedral and a detail of the sixteenth century Fountain of Orion.

city alone. As if that was not enough, the Second World War inflicte more hard blows on the already mutilated city.

Messina, as we see it today, is a fine modern city, restored to its form splendour by a grid of wide, well-lit avenues, lined by buildings whic are strictly earthquake-resistant, in the context of an extremely symmetr cal and linear city layout. Although very little remains of its architectur wonders and the considerable ruins that existed of its very ancient pas it is a city of great interest for its art and is surrounded by a region great natural beauty, with fine landscapes. It is a base for very interestir trips into a province rich in reminders of the past, a magnetic commerci centre and an important port for traffic between Sicily and the rest Italy.

The most typical folk festivities include the procession on Good Frida and the Vascelluzzo at Corpus Domini, the Sfilata dei Giganti (Processio of the Giants, in August), an allegorical representation of the foundir

The Church of the SS. Annunziata dei Catalani, begun in the twelfth century.

of the city, with huge equestrian statues followed by the racing Berbers, and the procession of the Vara (August), which symbolizes the mystery of the Assumption. Via Garibaldi, in the centre of the city, is the meeting place of the people of Messina. In Via Santa Cecilia a picturesque fish market is held daily; fresh fish, just caught, are offered by loud-voiced vendors. Fruit and vegetables are also sold here. Another daily market is held in Via Giostra; on sale there we can find clothes of all kinds, household articles and crafts items. These include ceramics, damasks and silks, embroideries and lace, the traditional Jew's harps called locally marranzanu, porcelain, cloth and puppets.

Duomo - The present appearance of the splendid Cathedral is the result of relatively recent rebuilding after the severe damage it suffered during the bombing of 1943; the church had already been rebuilt after the earthquake of 1908. The imposing building, flanked by a powerful and elegant bell tower, looks on to the Piazza Duomo where the Fountain of Orion stands. The original church was built in the second half of the twelfth century by the Norman king Roger II, replacing a previous Medieval building.

Of the **façade**, the only part belonging to the original building is the lower portion with inlays in relief representing scenes of ethnographical and historical interest. The rich and elegant portals are Gothic and the middle one, crowned by a tall carved spire, has at both sides lions supporting on their backs fine spiral columns. The side doors are from the sixteenth century, while the triple apse is quite impressive.

The **interior** has the form of a basilica with the nave divided from the aisles by columns supporting ogival arches. Almost entirely rebuilt, it has a wooden ceiling with original designs. On the right side, the first altar is adorned by a statue of the Baptist, a sixteenth century work by A.Gagini. Between the nave and the aisle we can see the Bellorado tomb, attributed to T.B.Mazzola (sixteenth century). Near the pilaster on the right, in the presbytery, is the De Tabiatis tomb, a work by the Sienese artist G.di Gregorio (fourteenth century). The mosaics in the apse, of thirteenth century origin, have been much altered by remodellings. Near the door, on the left side, is a fifteenth century bas-relief of the Penance of St. Jerome. The Cathedral organ is particularly imposing and complex. The **Crypt** lies under the apse and transept and in the seventeenth century formed the Church of Santa Maria.

Of great interest is the **Treasury**, which has been arranged in showcases and consists of fourteenth to seventeenth century chalices, twelfth to seventeenth century reliquiaries, eighteenth century bronze candelabra, valuable embroideries in gold and silver (seventeenth century), silk copes and chasubles (eighteenth century), rings, seals, rich mitres, illumined corals, silver vases (seventeenth-eighteenth centuries), paintings from the Byzantine age and other valuable objects and furnishings. A story in itself is the very unusual **Bell tower**, several times ruined by earthquakes and rebuilt according to the original Norman model. It is topped by a spire with four pinnacles around it and possesses an admirable clockwork mechanism commissioned by Bishop Paino and inaugurated in 1933. Its unusual moving figures represent subjects connected with religion, astronomy and local history.

Church of the Santissima Annunziata dei Catalani - This church was originally built in the Norman period, in the second half of the twelfth century, but it was remodelled in the following century. The cupola, transept and apse of the present building preserve the original structures. The **façade** goes back to the thirteenth century and has a central portal in the shape of an arch, with other portals to the sides each crowned by an architrave and a lancet window. The church, which was used as a royal chapel in the time of the Aragonese, was later used as a foundlings' hospital. In the sixteenth century it became a Dominican church and later accommodated a confraternity of Catalan merchants, which gave it its name. The **interior** has an aisled nave divided by columns with a barrel and cross vault, and reveals a mixture of influences, Arab, Roman and Lombard.

Church of San Francesco d'Assisi - Among the finest religious buildings in Messina, this church was seriously damaged by a fire in the second half of the last century and almost completely razed by the disastrous earthquake of 1908. However, in spite of repeated alterations over the centuries, the church still retains the appearance of a thirteenth century building. The original church was built in Norman times, with Sicilian-Arab features. We are surprised by the elegant and impressive exterior of the triple apse with its unusual crowning of Guelph battlements. On the right side is an ogival portal remaining from the original building.

Monastery of Montevergine - The church in this complex preserves an admirable monstrance, as well as eighteenth century chalices which are some of the most valuable articles in the Treasury. We should notice also the Sarcophagus of Beata Eustochia (fifteenth century).

Church of San Giovanni di Malta - This building is in Sicilian Baroque style, but seems to go back originally to the time of St.Placido, who was martyred there together with his brothers when the church of that time was destroyed by Muslims. Toward the end of the seventeenth century, the church was entrusted to the Knights of Jerusalem.

Church of Santa Maria degli Alemanni - The origins of this church go back to the first half of the thirteenth century, when it was built by the Teutonic Knights. It is a typical example of the architecture of the Swabian period, with strong Gothic characteristics. Unfortunately, when it was rebuilt after the earthquake its original structure was not respected; it had in any case been sacrificed by the dubious decisions of city planners.

Fountain of Orion - This is a masterpiece by the Florentine artist Fra' Giovanni Angelo da Montorsoli (sixteenth century); the admirable statue of the mythical founder of the city stands at the top of a pedestal formed by two basins separated and supported by mythological figures, which rises from a larger, polygonal basin enlivened by statues and allegorical representations of the *Tiber*, the *Nile*, the *Ebro* and the *Camaro*.

Monument to Don John of Austria - This is the work of the sculptor Andrea Calamech of Carrara (second half of the sixteenth century), and was inspired by the naval victory of Lepanto, which is portrayed in the admirable bronze bas-reliefs below the statue of the man who defeated the Turks.

The façade of the thirteenth century Church of San Francesco.

Fountain of Neptune - A sixteenth century work by Montorsoli. Quite badly damaged in the last century, it has been considerably restored and remodelled. At present Neptune stands on a pedestal rising out of a marble basin with the figures of Scylla and Charybdis in chains. The statue of Neptune brandishing his trident, and that of Scylla, are faithful nineteenth century copies of the originals in the National Museum.

Fort of San Salvatore - A sixteenth century fort built by the Spanish at the farthest tip of the peninsula of San Ranieri which gives the port its sickle shape. It is topped by a tall column with the statue of the Virgin Blessing.

Palace of Justice - A pompous building put up after the earthquake by the architect Marcello Piacentini. The imitation of the Doric style and the chariot over the façade remind us of features popular in the architecture of the Fascist period.

Regional Museum - The museum is in the rooms of what used to be the *Mellingoff Spinning Mill*, and contains interesting archaeological, medieval and modern art exhibits.

Cambria Zoological Museum - Intersting for its collection of vertebrates, insects and molluscs.

The Aquarium - The city aquarium, housed in the *Villa Mazzini*, has examples of fish fauna of the Mediterranean area and in particular of the Strait of Messina. There is also an interesting *Museum of Marine Fauna.*

Surrounding Area - *La Badiazza* is the name given to the Benedictine Monastery which was also known as *S. Maria della Valle*. The building, founded in the 13th century, was totally abandoned in the 16th century. In the architectural ruins we can still see remains of the fine ogival arches and the ornamental capitals in the style of the period between and Roman. Parts of the former Benedictine **Monastery of San Placido Calonerò** are still standing; the Cloister is in a good state of conservation. The original structure, built in the first half of the 15th century, was vast and a was inhabited by monks until the earlu 17th century.
The splendid beach at **Mortelle**, on the Strait of Messina, is a favourite seaside resort.
In the immediate surroundings are the so-called **Laghi di Ganzirri** (Ganzirri Lakes) - a picturesque fishing locality on the road leading to the **Punta del Faro**, the ancient Capo Peloro, where we find the huge infrastructure of the long-distance power line linking Sicily to the mainland.

Regional Museum: Madonna with Child, sixteenth century work attributed to Laurana, and Saint Catherine of Alexandria, work of an unknown follower of Laurana from Messina.

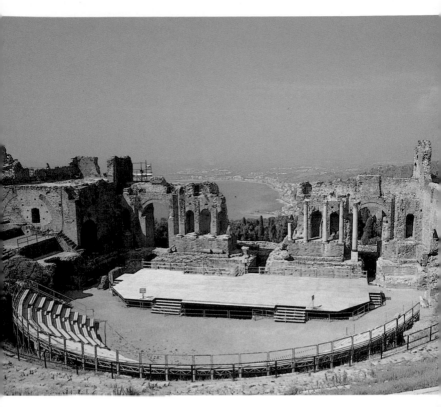

The Greek-Roman theatre, built in the third century B.C.

TAORMINA

Almost at the border of the province of Catania lies Taormina, on the slopes of Mount Tauro, in a very charming and panoramic spot that makes it one of the chief glories of Sicily. Because of its particularly fortunate micro-climate and its splendid natural situation, on a hill terrace overlooking the Ionian coast with the majestic and spectacular Etna as a backdrop, and owing also to the vastness of its historical, cultural and archaeological heritage, it is one of the places most visited by tourists in the whole island, a winter resort and a very important centre for holidaying. The town possesses refined and practical hotel and lodging facilties, extending to the beaches of **Isola Bella**, **Mazzarò** and **Spisone**, which are connected to the centre also by a cable car.

Greek in origin, *Tauromenion* grew up in the fourth century B.C. as a result of the decline of the Chalcidian colony of Naxos, even if it seems certain that when the first centre was founded Sicels were also present. It soon became part of the sphere of influence of Syracuse, and remained faithful to that city until the first Roman colonization, around the third century B.C. When Syracuse declined, Taormina became the capital of Byzantine Sicily, up to the time of the Arab conquest, at the beginning of the tenth century; it subsequently recovered its prosperity under the Normans.

Outstanding popular festivities of the town include the Festival of the Sicilian Cart, which is held in May, and the Summer performances in the Greek Theatre. The locality is known also for its flourishing crafts (pottery, porcelain, straw, wicker-work, cloth, lace, embroidery); we should make a special mention of the "firrizzi", a sort of small stool made of wood, easy to carry about and of obvious peasant origin, and the "sfilato" (pulled thread), a particular kind of Sicilian embroidery which enhances table mats and cloths, clothes and towels. Some pipes, called locally "friscaletti", made of reeds with rough engravings, are also typical. Other

Piazza del Duomo: the thirteenth century Cathedral and Baroque fountain.

craft activities include marble inlaying. Very beautiful works made of precious polychrome marbles (Sicilian Yellow, Lapislazuli, Taormina Red, Serpentine Green, Carrara Bardiglio, Pakistan Onyx, Levanto Red) can be bought at the workshop of the sculptor Gigi Samperi in Contrada Bianca (Castelmola road). The cosmopolitan crowd staying in the little town take their walks on the central Corso Umberto, where there are also numberless little craftsmen's workshops with an excellent selection of local products (especially fine are the coral and lava stone necklaces) and souvenirs for tourists. At Taormina, as in many other centres on the island, the typical Sicilian puppet shows are held.

The **Greek Theatre** is without question the most important feature for sight-seers, also because of its very fortunate natural setting, with splendid views toward the Calabrian coast, the Ionian coast of Sicily and the spectacular volcanic cone of Etna. The Theatre as we find it today is undoubtedly of the Roman period (second century B.C.); it was superimposed on earlier, similar structures of the Hellenistic period. The ancient Greek origins of the complex are evidenced by some inscriptions on the steps and the remains of a little temple which was sacrificed by the Romans when they enlarged the auditorium. The theatre of Taormina, second in size as far as Sicily is concerned only to that of Syracuse, shows signs of the alterations made so that gladiatorial shows could be held there. Of the two tiers of columns that must once have stood on the stage only a few pieces remain, replaced in an upright position during an awkward attempt at restoration in the last century.

Adjacent to the Theatre is the **Antiquarium** where archaeological finds of great interest are exhibited: there are epigraphs and sculptures, among the latter a *torso* copying a Greek original, a *woman's head* in marble of the Hellenistic period and a sarcophagus of the same material.

The remains of **Baths** of the Imperial period, consisting of three large rooms and several smaller ones, have come to light on the site of the ancient **Forum**, which is the present Piazza Vittorio Emanuele.

The **Naumachia** was probably a monumental nymphaeum built in the Imperial age, when the city was enriched by many public works. The present appearance of this structure is a wall with large apsed niches and a cistern behind it in a very poor state of repair.

Lastly, the vestiges of ancient Taormina include the **Odeon**, a covered theatre of the Imperial period, dating from the second century A.D. The auditorium, which is built of brick, consists of five small blocks, while the stage is backed by an ancient temple, partially incorporated into the Church of Santa Caterina, built much later; it is still not known to what god the temple was dedicated.

The **Palazzo Corvaia** is a fifteenth century building constructed for the meetings of the first parliament on the island. It has a battlemented facade enhanced by lancet windows and a fine portal in Catalan Gothic

A detail of the "Badia Vecchia", built in the fifteenth century.

style; there is a Latin inscription on the cornice. The small courtyard is charming.

The **Duomo** was originally built in the thirteenth century, but substantially altered during the Renaissance. The simple facade, which has three sections, is topped by a battlemented crowning. On the right side is a portal of Gothic appearance (sixteenth century), while the left side has a fifteenth century portal. The interior is divided into a nave and two aisles by large columns supporting ogival arches. On the second altar from the left is the statue of St.Agatha, a sixteenth century work attributed to the sculptor M.Montanini. On the right side we should notice a fifteenth century Visitation by A.Giuffré, a Madonna and Child with Saints by Antonello de Saliba (sixteenth century) and an alabaster sculpture of the Virgin (fifteenth century), in the chapel to the right of the high altar. In front of the building is a seventeenth century **fountain** in Baroque style with mythological figures, which is the emblem of the city. The busy

A view of Palazzo Corvaja and the entrance to Palazzo of the Dukes of Santo Stefano, both from the fifteenth century.

A view of the Odeon, a covered theatre from the second century A.D.

main street is the **Corso Umberto**, which provides a lively promenade for tourists and is lined with elegant shops and restaurants. Following this street we come to the scenic Piazza 9 Aprile, where the former **Church of Sant'Agostino**, a Gothic building of the fifteenth century, still stands; further on is the **Torre dell'Orologio** (Clock Tower), with a gate in it (**Porta di Mezzo**) leading to an area of great architectural and artistic interest, with many typically medieval features.

The **Badia Vecchia**, known also as *Badiazza*, is an evocative building in the form of a tower rising above the houses of the town. Built in the fifteenth century, it is a pleasing, square building which has been considerably restored. It is crowned by Ghibelline battlements, below which is a series of very fine ogival lancet windows; in the upper part they rest on a band of lava rock and pumice inlays.

The **Palazzo Ciampoli** goes back to the first half of the fifteenth century and is in typically Catalan Gothic style; the facade is lightened by a row of elegant lancet windows.

The **Palazzo of the Dukes of Santo Stefano** was the home of the De Spuches family, who called themselves Princes of Galati. The fourteenth to fifteenth century building has stylistic similarities to the Badia Vecchia and is marked by the rows of decorative lancet windows on the second floor, while the first floor has small trefoil arches. We should notice the decorative strip that completes the building at the top, made of lava rock and pumice inlay.

A characteristic feature of Taormina is the **Albergo San Domenico**, a hotel in a converted monastery building, of which the pleasant sixteenth century cloister and some of the interior decorations remain. Of the adjacent church of the same name, which was ruined by bombing in the Second World War, only the Baroque bell tower (sixteenth century) has been preserved.

Just outside the **Porta Messina** is the small **Church of San Pancrazio**, below which substantial remains of a Hellenistic temple have been found. Some inscriptions found inside it support the theory that it was dedicated to the cult of Isis and Serapis.

A pleasant walk along a track with fine views leads to the powerful medieval **Castle**, built at the top of Mount Tauro where the ancient acropolis once rose. From the top of the castle we can admire a wide and beautiful view.

The most important sea resorts of this part of the Ionian coast include **Letojanni**, the already mentioned **Mazzarò**, with its beautiful sickle-shaped beach, and above all **Giardini-Naxos**.

GIARDINI NAXOS

This enchanting seasonal and bathing resort with excellent tourist facilities has developed on the site of the ancient Greek colony of *Naxos*, founded in the eighth century B.C. and destroyed by the Syracusans three centuries later. What remains of the ancient settlement are substantial vestiges of the **walls**, dating from the sixth century B.C., some **gates** and a **tower**, besides the space that must have been occupied by a vast **sanctuary**. In this large area an ancient temple probably dedicated to the cult of Aphrodite has been identified (seventh to fifth centuries B.C.). Also in this area an **altar** and two **kilns**, probably connected with the sanctuary, have come to light. Another section of the archaeological area is occupied by the ruins of the city built to replace the one destroyed in 476 B.C.; remains of **temples** and artisans' **workshops** (those of makers of clay vases and statues) have been found here. The numerous finds from the area (pottery, clay objects, sculptures, terracottas, architectural fragments) are displayed in the ***Archaeological Museum of Naxos***, which is situated in the former Bourbon Fort on Cape Schisò.

Panorama of the port of Giardini-Naxos and a view of Isola Bella.

MILAZZO

This town rises at the eastern end of the gulf of the same name, at the base of a peninsula projecting into the waters of the Tyrrhenian sea. Archaeological finds provide proof that the area was first settled by humans in extremely ancient times; there are traces of necropolises dating from the fourteenth century B.C. Because of its strategic importance, the town was always a centre of military interest. A town was built on the present site around the eighth century B.C. by the Chalcidians (there had already been Sicel settlements there), as a stronghold for Messina. Near this ancient town of *Mylae*, the Carthaginians were defeated by the Romans in a naval battle in the third century B.C.; subsequently Sextus Pompeius was defeated there during the civil war. An important administrative centre during the Arab and Norman ages, the town retained its powers under the Spanish also. In 1860 Garibaldi won an important victory over the Bourbons there, during his memorable campaign.

The most important of the popular religious festivities of the town is the Via Crucis on Easter Saturday, with figures in costume.

The **Castle** in its present form goes back to the fifteenth to sixteenth centuries, when the Spanish further fortified the previous thirteenth century structure built by Frederick II of Swabia.

In the highest part of the town, near the castle and the ring walls, stands the **Duomo Vecchio** (Old Cathedral), which is a seventeenth century building in Renaissance style.

The **Church (Sanctuary) of San Francesco di Paola** contains a fine Madonna and Child by Gagini.

In the **Duomo Nuovo** (New Cathedral) are preserved interesting paintings by the sixteenth century artist Antonello de Saliba. We will mention St.Roch, St.Peter, St.Paul, and St.Thomas Aquinas, in the apse. The Adoration of the Child is by the same artist, while the Annunciation and a St.Nicholas are attributed to the fifteenth century painter A.Giuffré.

We should also see the Gothic **Palazzo dei Giudici** and the **Palazzo Municipale** which contains mementos of the Risorgimento, a well-stocked library and various paintings.

The narrow strip of land on which Milazzo lies.

An evocative aerial view of the Sanctuary of the Black Madonna and the typical tongues of golden sand round Tindari.

TINDARI

Tindari is an area of great archaeological interest at the western end of the bay between Cape Tindari and the Cape of Milazzo. The solitary situation of the place, in one of the most evocative and panoramic settings on the coast of Messina, gives it the ambience of an enchanted island, dotted with the monumental vestiges of its past.

Founded in the first half of the fourth century B.C. to celebrate the victory of the Syracusans over Carthage, it was known as *Tyndaris*, and was a loyal ally first of its mother city and then, from the third century B.C., of Rome, which it always supported in its long military struggle with Carthage. In the Imperial age it became the *Colonia Augusta Tyndaritanorum*, and later suffered recurrent natural disasters, landslides and earthquakes, which led to a relentless decline culminating in its destruction at the hand of the Arabs (ninth century).

We can still see substantial remains of the ancient **walls**, some sections of which are the original city walls, while other portions are of later date. There are two gates in the walls; the principal one is situated slightly below the present village.

The outstanding feature of the ruins is the **Greek Theatre**, which dates from the fourth century B.C., and where excavation and restoration were begun in the first half of the last century. The auditorium, which is divided into eleven blocks by ten small flights of steps, rests on the side of the hill and opens out toward the view of the sea. In the Roman period the orchestra space was considerably remodelled so that gladiatorial shows could be held there.

Near a vaulted structure, improperly supposed to be a basilica but almost certainly a monumental entrance porch, is a vast block of buildings on several levels, known as **Isolato IV**. The lower levels are occupied by the remains of Roman houses and shops (*tabernae*). The upper level consists of the remains of the **Baths**, dating from the second century A.D. The Baths are divided into different rooms: the Frigidarium, where the pool is decorated with mosaics, the Tepidarium, with mosaics in the floor and vestiges of the heating system.

In the **Museum** beside the Theatre we can see some interesting finds from the excavations. In the outer porch are fragments that once adorned the stage of the Theatre.

In **Room I** the chronology of the settlement is explained in topographical material and information about the excavations and the work of restoration.

Room II accommodates architectural fragments, and Greek inscriptions and sculptures probably from a not yet identified temple.

Room III contains commemorative sculptures and a gigantic head of Augustus.

In **Room IV** we find various objects from the Greek and Roman periods, a terracotta Corinthian capital and other materials from the excavations.

In **Room V** are exhibited finds from prehistoric times, dated as of the Bronze Age, ceramic and clay materials from the Greek period, finds from the Greco-Roman necropolis and fragments of decorations from the houses.

In modern Tindari, which probably grew up on the site of the ancient *agorà*, we should visit the **Santuario**, a modern building rising on the site of the acropolis of the ancient settlement, near a smaller sixteenth century sanctuary now out of bounds to the public. In this sanctuary an image of a Black Virgin is worshipped; it is held to be Byzantine and almost certainly of Eastern origin.

AEOLIAN ISLANDS

The Aeolian archipelago (in modern Italian "Isole Eolie" or "Lipari") lies off the coast of Milazzo and is made up of seven major islands and a series of rocks and islets. The main geological component of these islands is volcanic rock and lava from several quite separate eras; the result is wild coasts with sheer cliffs above the sea, a landscape of fascinating beauty enhanced by innumerable small craters and still active volcanos. The serene luminosity of the Aeolian landscape is the fruit of the complex intermingling of the elements composing it, the wild, burnt lava slopes, the brilliant blue waters which vary, according to the light, toward evocative shades of emerald green, the colourful and variegated image of the archipelago as a whole, where the bitter smell of volcanic sulphur mixes with the fresh, scented sea breezes.

The first settlements on the island date from prehistoric times. Around 4000 B.C. Neolithic peoples settled on Lipari to exploit its rich obsidian deposits. There is evidence that as early as the eighteenth century B.C. Aeolian peoples had established there bases on the important trade routes passing through the Straits of Messina. The placename is attributed to them, although others connect it with Homeric tradition and the myth of Homer. The flourishing Aeolian civilization declined because of a sudden depopulation around the tenth century B.C. Toward the sixth century B.C. Greek colonizers of Doric extraction repopulated the archipelago; at the time of the Punic Wars (third century B.C.) it became a strategic stronghold for the Carthaginians, and a fierce battle occurred in its waters between the Carthaginians and Romans (257 B.C.).

With the coming of the Romans the settlement declined considerably although it was used for its hot springs and for sea bathing, and remained important as a sea-port and in naval strategy. In the early Middle Ages Lipari was the seat of bishops and a religious centre of great importance within a context rich in traditions and legends. In the ninth century Lipari was raided by Muslims; this was the first of the long series of attacks by pirates that marked the Medieval period on the archipelago. It revived in the Norman period, thanks to a community of Benedictine monks, and from then on shared the fortunes of Sicily and the Kingdom of Naples

Top: an enchanting view of the cliffs and a port on the island of Lipari; center: the Island of Vulcano; bottom: a view of Filicudi.

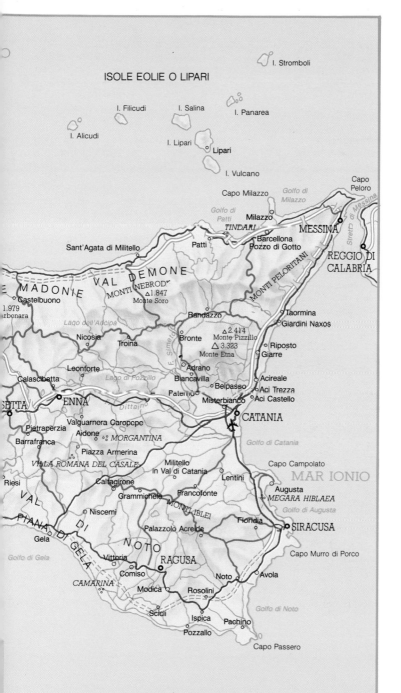

INDEX